Answers to Exercises
in
A Short Course IN Grammar

A Course in the Grammar of Standard Written English

Paul J. Hopper
Carnegie Mellon University

W. W. Norton & Company

New York / London

0-393-97408-1

6 7 8 9 0

CONTENTS

PREFACE

The exercises at the end of the chapters in *A Short Course in Grammar* are intended to provide practice in the use of the grammatical concepts introduced in the text. The sentences that appear in them were therefore designed to be representative of clear examples of the concept. Thus, in distinguishing adjectives from the *-en* forms of verbs in 6.2 you will find less ambiguity than is often present in real discourse. Still, instructors should be prepared for students to find interpretations they had not thought of and that are not represented in the solutions offered. Furthermore, instructors may not agree with all of my own judgments as they appear in this manual. To discuss with a class their reasons for differing would be a valuable experience for the students.

A word about the diagrams. Limitations in both the length of the manual and the layout of the printed page have made it impossible to give complete examples from all the exercises where diagrams are asked for. I have tried to mitigate this lack by adding (I hope) helpful comments about details that were omitted or suppressed and by trying to ensure that the diagrams given were representative of the type of sentence in the exercise as a whole. Incidentally, students may ask to see a diagram of some sentence picked out of other exercises; mine do this frequently. It might be as well to emphasize at the outset that in a single course they can only learn to diagram a very restricted and simplified set of sentences. The sentences to be diagrammed have been constructed carefully and with much trial and error to ensure that they conform to the diagramming concepts already introduced at that point. Sentences in other exercises have not been designed with diagramming in mind, and it is not appropriate to assign them as diagramming exercises or to use them as diagramming examples in class.

A Short Course in Grammar is written for the general pedagogy of students who aspire to be skilled writers, not as an introduction to syntax or linguistics. Grammar these days, usually called syntax, is a highly complex and technical field. *A Short Course in Grammar* is offered in the belief that something very useful can be learned in a single academic term.

Paul Hopper
August 1998

EXERCISE ANSWERS: CHAPTER 1

Exercise 1.1

(Some items for class discussion) Some of the following statements reflect misunderstandings or are inadequate as they stand. Change or amplify them so that they reflect the discussion in Chapter 1.

1. Swedish and Icelandic are Germanic languages. (Can you be more specific than this?)

   Swedish and Iceleandic are both members of the North Germanic sub-branch of Germanic.

2. The older Germanic languages evolved into the present-day spoken Germanic languages. (Give examples. Did any of the older Germanic languages fail to survive into the present day?)

   Old English, or Anglo-Saxon, evolved into present-day English; Old Norse is the ancestor language of Icelandic and Norwegian, for example.

3. "The German for 11 and 12 is *elf* and *zwölf* (from which the English was presumably derived)."—Leonard Gillman, cited in the *New York Times*, Aug. 6, 1995, 7E. (Give Dr. Gillman, an eminent mathematician, some help with his linguistics!)

   German is not the source from which English is derived. The words for "eleven" and "twelve" in German go back to the same Germanic roots as the English words, but the English words are not descended from German.

4. Old Norse, Gothic, and Anglo-Saxon are all early representatives of the Proto-Germanic language family. (How is the term "Proto-Germanic" being misused here?)

   The term "Proto-Germanic" refers not to all the members of the Germanic family, but to the reconstructed ancestor language of the entire family.

5. Proto-Germanic is the hypothetical ancestor language of the Germanic language family, reconstructed on the basis of linguistic evidence taken from all the languages of the family.

   This is true. The oldest recorded stages of Germanic, such as Old English, Gothic, and Old Norse, provide the most reliable evidence for what Proto-Germanic must have been like.

6. Roman, Greek, and Cyrillic are the names of alphabets.

   True.

7. The Slavic languages are written in the Cyrillic alphabet. (Of which Slavic languages is this not true?)

This is true of some Slavic languages—for example, Russian and Bulgarian. But other Slavic languages, for example Czech and Polish, are written in the Latin alphabet.

8. *Ain't* is a dialect form of *isn't*. (Is *ain't* really a dialect—regionally restricted form?)

   Ain't is not a dialect form—it is found in all parts of the English-speaking world. It should be avoided in formal writing.

9. Writing is a graphic representation of speech. (Refer to the section in 1.3 on the relationship of writing to speech.)

   Written language and spoken language are so different that it is better to think of them as distinct languages. However, the formal registers of spoken English—for example, lectures, panel discussions and speeches—may closely resemble the written language.

10. Studying English grammar will help us speak more correctly. (In discussing this statement, don't forget to talk about the implications of the notion of "speaking correctly"!)

    Studying English grammar will help us be aware of the conventions for writing correct sentences. But correctness in formal writing is not the same as correctness in speech. In fact there is no clear way to explain what it means to "speak correctly." English is a very diverse language, and there is no single standard by which to identify grammatical correctness once we depart from formal writing. (The supposed rules for "correct English" are all derived from the conventions of writing.)

Exercise 1.2

Numerous other language families have been studied. One of these is the Romance family, whose members include French, Italian, Spanish, and Portuguese. Go to an encyclopedia or other source, find other examples of Romance languages, and construct a family tree similar to the one we gave for Germanic in Chapter 1. The proto-language for the Germanic family (Proto-Germanic) does not exist in actual documents; in what important respect is the proto-language for the Romance family different?

Proto-Romance was apparently a dialect of Latin brought to parts of the Roman Empire by the armies of Rome. Since Latin is well known, scholars are much closer to the proto-language of the Romance family than they are to Proto-Germanic and can say much more about the common source of the Romance languages.

Exercise 1.9

Identify the genre. What word choices and grammatical forms provide the best clues?

1. He is best remembered for his performance as a streetsweeper in the 1955 Broadway musical *Starlit Nights*.

   *The phrase **best remembered for** and the 1955 date may suggest to you an obituary. Another possibility is a newspaper or magazine article about the theater or cinema.*

2. Profits were up slightly in the third quarter, but not enough to recoup the severe losses resulting from the natural disasters earlier in the year.

   *A number of phrases suggest a financial report of some kind (**profits were up, third quarter, recoup the severe losses**).*

3. We beseech thee, O Lord, to preserve and defend those we love.

   *The use of the archaic pronoun **thee**, the verb **beseech**, and the phrase **O Lord** point to a prayer.*

4. For the third night running, UN relief convoys have been turned back by heavy shelling.

   *The use of the verb phrase **have been turned back** suggests a news report. Notice how the use of **have** makes this a recent happening, as opposed to **were turned back**, which might be part of a history.*

5. After a reception in the Tivoli Hotel, the couple will fly to Majorca for their honeymoon.

   *The vocabulary **reception, couple, honeymoon** identify the topic as a wedding; the future **will** tells us that the wedding has not yet taken place, and so this is undoubtedly a wedding announcement.*

6. The alleged suspect was apprehended while attempting to conceal himself in a freight elevator.

   *It reads as if the author is striving for great care in formulating the statement. **Alleged suspect**, for example—one can be an alleged perpetrator, or a suspect in a crime, but can one be an alleged suspect? The unnecessarily long expressions (**was apprehended while attempting to conceal himself** = "he was caught while trying to hide") likewise point to circumspection of the kind often necessary in police work, where public statements may later have to be repeated in court.*

7. Stir into the melted butter one tbsp. refined flour and heat until almost brown. Add the sauce slowly to the flour mixture.

   *The sequence of imperatives (**stir, heat, add**) and the cooking vocabulary point unambiguously to a recipe. Note also the abbreviation **tbsp.** for tablespoon, and the dropping of the pronoun **it** after the verb **heat**.*

8. Anyway, gotta go now, but Jack sends his love, and we'll see you next month in San Diego, I hope.

   *Probably a letter or e-mail message. The absence of the subject pronoun before **gotta**, the form **gotta** itself (a humorous way of representing the* *spoken form of **got to**), the conjunction **but**, and the way that **I hope** is tacked on at the end—all point to an informal and rapidly written communication.*

9. If a document you are working on is part of a longer document, you can use the Number From option under Footnotes in the Document command to set a start number. Be sure to turn off the Restart Each Section option if necessary.

   *The genre of the user's manual is well represented here. Note that, despite the technical vocabulary set with initial capitals, the authors have adopted a somewhat casual style (for example, **a document you are working on** rather than "on which you are working"). The use of the pronoun **you**, the imperative verb **turn**, and the phrase **be sure to** also has the effect of establishing a fairly close relationship with the reader, giving an impression of user-friendliness.*

10. Gone to class. Back 9:30. Don't forget to take dog out. Spaghetti sauce in fridge. Love, J.

    *A domestic note, left on a table or fixed to the refrigerator. The register is intimate: pronouns, auxiliary verbs and the verb **to be** (**have, will be, is**), and the articles **the** and **some** are dropped; sentences are brief, very concrete, and informative; the sign-off, **Love, J.**, is minimal. An extreme example of informal writing.*

Exercise 1.10

Convert all the sentences into a more formal register, such as, for example, an office memo or a published report. What changes in *content* do you find yourself wanting to make when you adapt them? Is there any material you might prefer not to express at all in the formal register?

Some suggestions are given in italics.

1. I wouldn't park back of that building if I was you.

   You are advised not to park your vehicle in the rear of the building.

2. Hate to hafta tell you this, but you know Chuck Kovak? The Big Enchilada of the whole outfit? Keeled over last night. Heart attack. Never knew what hit him. They got him to the ER, but he'd already croaked. I heard he was out on a binge with his drinking buddies.

   I am very sorry to inform you of the death of Charles Novak, the Chief Executive Officer of this organization. Mr. Novak suffered a massive heart attack last night while dining with friends. Although medical assistance arrived swiftly, he passed away in the ambulance on his way to the hospital.

3. If there's anything in the way of paperclips, stationery, notepads, that kind of thing, you need, just get ahold of Bud Rethke, he's the office manager around here.

Our office manager, Mr. George "Bud" Rethke, is in charge of all office supplies and can help you with any items of that nature you may need.

4. We just added a few drops of that stuff and the whole kaboodle started to bubble and seethe like you wouldn't believe.

   A small amount of the substance, when added, caused a vigorous effervescent reaction.

5. The whole area of the building catty-corner across the courtyard from us is gonna be off limits to us folks 'coz they're tearing everything down to build a snazzy new headquarters for the big cheeses.

   The area of the building diagonally across the courtyard from us is to be closed off during the demolition. After the site has been cleared, a new construction is planned to house the center of operations for our organization.

EXERCISE ANSWERS: CHAPTER 2

Exercise 2.1

Each of the items 1–4 below consists of a set of words and a pair of category names. For each item, place the words in one of three columns according to whether they belong unambiguously in one of the categories (columns I and II), or could plausibly belong to *either* of the categories named (column III). For each of the words in column III, make up two sentences exemplifying its use in each category. Here are some examples from item (1) by way of illustration:

I. NOUN	II. VERB	III. EITHER NOUN OR VERB
photo	misjudge	alarm

"alarm" as noun: We left the building when the alarm sounded.
"alarm" as verb: The earthquake warnings alarmed the population.

Answers:

1. *Noun and verb:* cat, squirrel, misjudge, violin, photo, arm, wrist, unlock, thumb, entertainment, carry, alarm

I. NOUN	II. VERB	III. EITHER NOUN OR VERB
photo, cat, violin, wrist, entertainment	misjudge, unlock, carry	squirrel, arm, thumb, alarm

Example sentences:

Squirrels hibernate until March/They squirreled away most of their profits

His arm was injured in the accident/They did not arm the campus police

She jabbed the portrait with her thumb/We thumbed a ride to Memphis

The earthquake forecast alarmed the population of the city/My alarm did not go off this morning

2. *Adjective and verb:* large, smooth, amaze, dry, calm, drunk, silence, renew, thin, red, force

I. ADJECTIVE	II. VERB	III. EITHER ADJECTIVE OR VERB
large, drunk, red	amaze, renew, force, silence	smooth, dry, calm, thin

Example sentences:

The surface was smooth/They poured oil on the water to smooth the waves

We gave them dry clothing/The hikers were drying their socks

The sea is fairly calm today/The trainers were trying to calm the dogs

A thin wire ran from the trigger to the door/You must thin the paint with turpentine

3. *Adjective and adverb:* deadly, heavy, poor, poorly, good, well, faster, early, late, soon

I. ADJECTIVE	II. ADVERB	III. EITHER ADJECTIVE OR ADVERB
deadly, heavy, poor, good	soon. "Poorly" is adverb-only for some speakers	faster, early, well, late. "Poorly" belongs to both categories for some speakers

Example sentences:

We wanted to catch a faster train/The bicycle will run faster if you oil the wheels

The mailman was early today/The plane landed early

The magnolias are late this year/Our mail was delivered late today

Mrs. Garcia is very poorly this morning/The class performed poorly on the test

4. *Preposition and conjunction:* and, although, during, since, while, except, of, but, after, near, until

I. PREPOSITION	II. CONJUNCTION	III. EITHER PREPOSITION OR CONJUNCTION
during, except, of, near	and, although, while, but	since, until, after

Example sentences:

Nancy has not been herself since the funeral/Since you missed the performance, you cannot write the review

Henry stayed in bed until noon/The guests remained seated until the president entered the room

After the ceremony, there was a barbecue/After they had removed the tree, a large hole was left in the flower beds

Exercise 2.2

In each of the following sentences, one item is italicized. Identify its category (part of speech).

1. There was not enough *oxygen* in the fish tank.

   noun

2. The children had been *flying* kites in the park.

   verb

3. He had gone to the movies *with* some of his friends.

   preposition

4. He was wearing a pink blazer *and* a green tie.

   conjunction

5. The eighteenth century was a *time* of intense reflection on the human condition.

   noun

6. An *ingeniously* contrived arrangement of string and tin cans guarded the entrance.

   adverb

7. *They* were coming for us at eight o'clock.

   pronoun

8. Someone asked me to hand *over* my passport.

   preposition

9. The books *were* fascinating.

   verb or *linking verb*

10. All the guests *were* leaving.

    auxiliary or *auxiliary verb*

Exercise 2.3

In the following sentences, underline the word or words that belong to the category or have the function indicated in parentheses after the sentence.

1. The toolshed behind the parking lot looked <u>cluttered</u>. (adjective)
2. I looked up the word in <u>an old dictionary</u>. (complement of preposition)
3. The "fast" train to Boston was <u>quite</u> slow. (adverb)
4. Besides Marty <u>and</u> me, a couple of flashy-looking guys, each with two bodyguards, were in the elevator. (coordinating conjunction)
5. Gary had a battered Mercedes that <u>had</u> seen better days. (auxiliary verb)
6. I will have another of <u>those</u> delicious Campari sodas, please. (demonstrative)
7. Apparently Fred had been <u>hallucinating</u> again. (verb)
8. These marginal sects are unlikely to influence <u>the</u> election. (article)
9. <u>Since</u> they have vented the nuclear reactors again, we will have to cancel our outdoor barbecue. (subordinating conjunction)
10. The editor maintains that <u>that</u> "that" that I used should be "which." (demonstrative)

EXERCISE ANSWERS: CHAPTER 3

Exercise 3.1

Underline the noun phrases which are the subjects of the following sentences.

1. <u>Some of the nation's leading economists</u> agreed with the committee's conclusions.
2. <u>The Lorentz transformations</u> are a system of equations.
3. <u>These equations</u> link the coordinates of events in different inertial frames.
4. <u>The nineteenth-century Dutch physicist H. A. Lorentz</u> devised the equations.
5. <u>The subject-predicate division</u> perhaps reflects the dualism of western thought.
6. <u>Temperatures in the polar regions</u> can be dangerously low.
7. <u>A sudden and dangerous downturn in the economy</u> startled the bankers.
8. <u>The unexpected failure of the electric fences</u> had made the dinosaur park a scary place to picnic.

9. <u>Our annual shipment of men's and women's winter clothing</u> will be arriving tomorrow.

10. <u>We</u> almost never went swimming in the polluted lake.

Exercise 3.2

Parts a and b may be ignored if you are confident that you understand the principle.

a. Go back to Exercise 3.1 and draw for each sentence a *form* diagram (tree diagram) similar to Diagram 3A, Alternative 1. Use the triangle convention to abbreviate the tree.

b. Then do the same using the underlining convention, with the *function* labels Subject and Predicate, as in Alternative 2.

c. Finally, for each sentence, combine the two diagrams into a unified form-function diagram.

Here are two sample diagrams:

1. Some of the nation's leading economists agreed with the committee's conclusions.

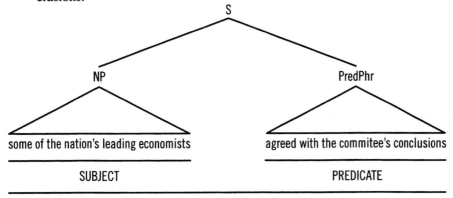

10. We almost never went swimming in the polluted lake.

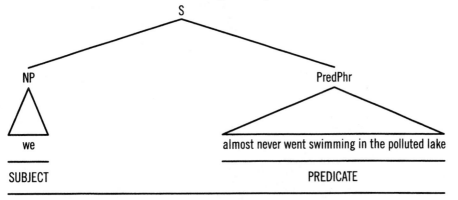

Exercise 3.3

For each of the following NPs, draw a complete form-function diagram starting with S as the highest node. Assume in each case that the NP is the subject of the sentence.

A few examples are given. The remainder of the exercise can be modeled on these.

1. terrifying images

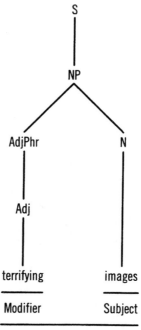

2. they

3. undrinkable Belgian beer

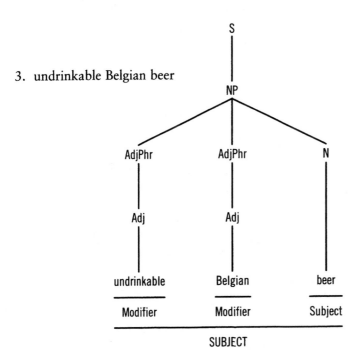

```
                           S
                           |
                          NP
              _____/|_____
          AdjPhr      AdjPhr            N
            |            |              |
           Adj          Adj             |
            |            |              |
       undrinkable    Belgian         beer
       _____   _____        _____
        Modifier     Modifier       Subject
       _____
                      SUBJECT
```

6. an almost unbelievably ingenious contraption

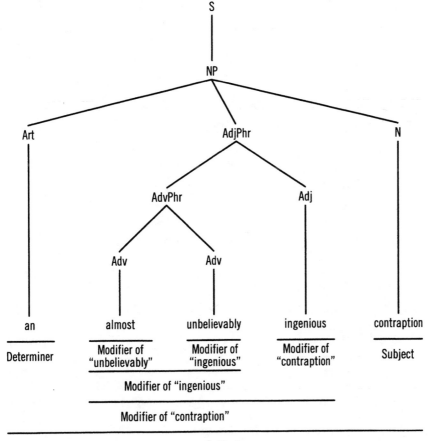

```
                              S
                              |
                             NP
        _____/|_____
      Art                  AdjPhr                      N
       |            _____/  _____                |
       |         AdvPhr            Adj                  |
       |        __/  \__            |                   |
       |      Adv      Adv          |                   |
       |       |        |           |                   |
       an    almost  unbelievably ingenious        contraption
      ____   _____  _____ _____        _____
   Determiner Modifier of  Modifier of  Modifier of   Subject
             "unbelievably" "ingenious" "contraption"
             _____
                Modifier of "ingenious"
             _____
                     Modifier of "contraption"
       _____
                              Subject
```

11

Exercise 3.4

Draw form-function diagrams of the following sentences, using the triangle convention to abbreviate the phrases identified in parentheses.

Again, sample diagrams are given on which the others can be based.

2. That incredibly scary movie was playing. (Predicate, Adjectival Phrase)

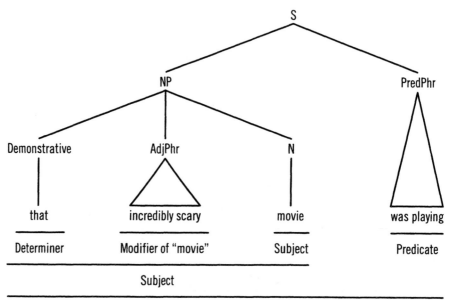

3. Jenny, Cheryl, Tracy, Marvin, and Justin have already left. (Subject, Predicate)

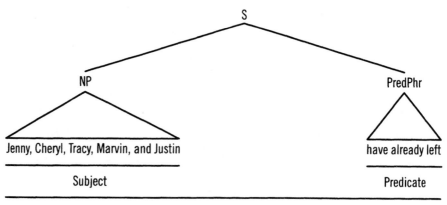

4. One of those policemen that stopped us yesterday was at the mall.
   (Subject, Predicate)

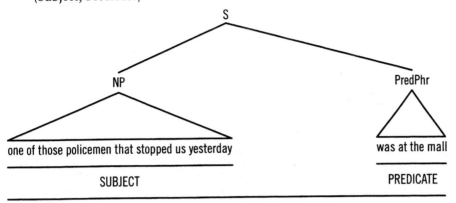

Exercise 3.5

The following diagram has a set of true/false questions after it. Inspect the diagram carefully and answer the questions with T or F.

1. Dem (demonstrative) is a nonbranching node. ___*T*___
2. NP dominates AdjPhr and Dem. ___*T*___
3. The Determiner is a Demonstrative. ___*T*___
4. AdjPhr dominates Adj and Dem. ___*F*___
5. NP immediately dominates Dem. ___*T*___
6. "Strangely evocative fragrance" is a subject. ___*F*___
7. "That strangely evocative" is a phrase modifying "fragrance." ___*F*___
8. AdjPhr is a branching node. ___*T*___
9. "Strangely" modifies "evocative fragrance." ___*F*___
10. AdjPhr immediately dominates Adv and Adj. ___*T*___

EXERCISE ANSWERS: CHAPTER 4

Exercise 4.1

a. Convert the following statements into (closed) questions, and in doing so identify the NP that is the subject of the sentence. Underline the *whole subject* (i.e., the whole phrase that inverted with the auxiliary).

b. At the same time, identify the *auxiliary verb* with which the subject NP switches places.

c. In some of the sentences, you will have to use a trial-and-error procedure to find the exact beginning of the subject noun phrase. Put parentheses around any words that precede the subject in these sentences.

In the answer sentences, the subject NP is underlined and the auxiliary is in boldface.

1. That little kid from Kalamazoo with a blue ribbon in her hair will explain her theory to all these important scientists.

   *That little kid from Kalamazoo with a blue ribbon in her hair **will** explain her theory to all these important scientists.*

2. A bottle of the best Highland single-malt Scotch whiskey would make a nice present.

   *A bottle of the best Highland single-malt Scotch whiskey **would** make a nice present.*

3. They don't sell tickets to nonmembers.

   *They **don't** sell tickets to nonmembers.*

4. The day after tomorrow you could please help me get the piano up the steps.

   *(The day after tomorrow) you **could** please help me get the piano up the steps.*

5. The Buccaneers have reached the quarter-finals.

   *The Buccaneers **have** reached the quarter-finals.*

6. If it doesn't rain tomorrow, they are having a barbecue in the state park.

   *(If it doesn't rain tomorrow,) they **are** having a barbecue in the state park.*

7. When the workers come, they should fix the TV as well as take away the dishwasher.

   *(When the workers come,) they **should** fix the TV as well as take away the dishwasher.*

8. A course in basket-weaving does count for credit under the Creative Activity requirement.

   *A course in basket-weaving **does** count for credit under the Creative Activity requirement.*

9. After sunset astronomers will be able to see the new comet.

   *(After sunset) astronomers **will** be able to see the new comet.*

10. Just one of these new super-high density disks can hold the entire manuscript.

    *Just one of these new super-high density disks **can** hold the entire manuscript.*

11. If the electric fence were down, the dinosaurs would be able to reach the compound.

    (If the electric fence were down,) <u>*the dinosaurs*</u> ***would*** *be able to reach the compound.*

12. The new recruits are being trained properly.

    <u>*The new recruits*</u> *are being trained properly.*

13. Next year that professor of statistics who lost his shirt in Las Vegas might be spending his vacation in Orlando.

    (Next year) <u>*that professor of statistics who lost his shirt in Las Vegas*</u> ***might*** *be spending his vacation in Orlando.*

14. That battered old 1943 Ford with the silver hubcaps will make it up this steep hill.

    <u>*That battered old 1943 Ford with the silver hubcaps*</u> ***will*** *make it up this steep hill.*

Exercise 4.2

(For class discussion) In this exercise you are asked to make a stylistic judgment to distinguish between attempted sentences that are poorly constructed and effectively used sentence fragments. Identify those "sentences" that are grammatically incomplete but that still seem to be appropriate (if hackneyed!) in the context of the whole example. Comment on the registers and genres that seem especially hospitable to sentence fragments.

1. It happened one warm June evening. An evening heavy with the fragrance of jasmine and honeysuckle. The sort of evening that made you wish you were young again.

   The sentence fragments are motivated by the dramatic style.

2. Before turning on the ignition, press the gas pedal right to the floor and hold it down. For a few seconds.

   For a few seconds *is disconnected from its context and should be joined to the full sentence by dropping the period.*

3. Now Jack was gaining on him, and the finish line seemed miles away. He summoned up every last ounce of strength. Twenty more yards.

   The fragment ***twenty more yards*** *is motivated by being the inner thought of the competitor.*

4. Face on Mars "Portrait of Julius Caesar"—NASA Expert

   A newspaper headline, where fragments are normal.

5. The homeless man looked at him pitifully, but Salford ignored him and walked resolutely past. Didn't do any good to encourage them. No good at all. Obstructing the public sidewalks like that, harrassing responsible, hard-working citizens.

The fragments represent the thoughts of the character.

6. You wait until the kettle is boiling its head off. Then you pour the water onto the tea leaves. Right on top of them. While the water is still actually boiling.

   The fragments here are unmotivated and inappropriate for the formal written language.

7. The gala opening ceremony was canceled. Because of the tornado warning.

   A simple error of punctuation. The second clause should be attached to the first without a comma.

8. The aftershave with the fragrance that speaks to her. Cool. Bracing. And now with all-new doctor-recommended polypromethalone skin toner!

   A magazine ad or TV commercial, where full sentences are not expected.

9. The shipment is being held up for no good reason, and I suggest contacting the customs people in London. Immediately.

   There doesn't seem to be any good reason for this fragment. It should be linked to the full sentence with, at the most, a comma.

10. Down with capitalist exploiters and other enemies of the people!

    Slogans typically lack some of the trappings of the full sentence.

Exercise 4.3

Identify the following sentences from the point of view of their form as declaratives, interrogatives (open or closed), imperatives, sentence fragments, verbless interrogatives, exclamatives, or hortatives.

1. The covered casserole should be baked for 25 minutes at 375°F.

   declarative

2. Must I remove the plunger before tightening the wing nut?

   closed interrogative

3. Because of my asthma.

   sentence fragment

4. How long will you remain in Ulan Bator?

   open interrogative

5. Let's push the buttons for all 71 floors and then get out of the elevator!

   hortative

6. So help me God!

   exclamative

7. What about the third-quarter losses?

   verbless interrogative

8. Who put a piece of barbed wire in Buster Bottomley's bed?

   open interrogative

9. When the sauce has thickened, spoon it carefully over the scallops and orange slices.

   imperative

10. "World War II Bomber Found on Moon"—NASA Officials

    sentence fragment

11. Heaven forbid that he should wash the dishes for once!

    exclamative

12. What if Ms. Dulwitz sees us putting the toadstools in the stew?

    verbless interrogative

13. Don't you worry about Cobber Doogan!

    imperative

14. Would that it would rain for a week!

    exclamative

15. You must apologize to Aunt Agatha about the chewing gum.

    declarative

16. What to Do If Skweezit Does Not Boot.

    sentence fragment

17. Mr. Van Hefflin knows all the regulations by heart.

    declarative

18. Remember the time we sent a mouse up in the elevator to Niedermeyer's office?

    closed interrogative

19. Avoid those guys in double-breasted suits standing next to the car!

    imperative

20. How much is that army-issue bazooka in the window?

    open interrogative

EXERCISE ANSWERS: CHAPTER 5

Exercise 5.1

Here are some examples of sentences that contain precore phrases. Identify these phrases as *pre-adjuncts* or *adverbials*, and state whether they express the

17

writer's attitude, introduce a new topic, or state a time, place, manner, or circumstance for the sentence.

1. Astonishingly, Dr. Kromm accuses me of misusing my sources.
   pre-adjunct (expresses writer's attitude)
2. With a flourish, Mr. Samsonov produced a Lithuanian-English dictionary.
   adverbial of manner
3. The night before last a number of strange lights appeared in the sky.
   adverbial of time
4. During the chamber music concert, Mr. Leary ate candies with noisy wrappers.
   adverbial of time
5. As regards your memo of September 20, I will raise this matter with the board at their next meeting.
   pre-adjunct (introduces a new topic)
6. With considerable vigor, Lee hit a fly ball to center field.
   adverbial of manner
7. Tomorrow morning we will investigate those funny noises.
   adverbial of time
8. Brusquely, the border guard asked to see our passports.
   adverbial of manner
9. Concerning your inquiry about costume jewelry, we are sending you a catalog by express mail.
   pre-adjunct (introduces a new topic)
10. Yesterday our plan seemed flawless.
    adverbial of time

Exercise 5.3

Write beside each of the following sentences the formula selected from (1)–(5) below that sums up its basic structure. Some sentences have multiple possibilities (indicated by a number in parentheses after the sentence).

(1) S-V

   Example: *The dynamite exploded.*

(2) S-V-SC

   Example: *The pages of the manuscript had turned yellow.*

(3) S-V-DO

   Example: *The intense heat buckled the railroad tracks.*

(4) S-V-IO-DO

Example: *The owners paid the star performers enormous salaries.*

(5) S-V-DO-OC

Example: *The inflation made many people poor.*

Answers:

1. At the shopping mall Lisa bought a fancy key ring.
   S-V-DO
2. The asparagus were already cooking.
   S-V
3. The king made Little Mattie Grove a knight of the Round Table.
   S-V-DO-OC
4. The colors were fascinating.
   S-V-SC
5. Mr. Hollingsworth often used to get angry.
   S-V-SC
6. Little Mattie Grove made the king one of his fine rabbit pies.
   S-V-IO-DO
7. In the workshop, a skilled carpenter was finishing a table.
   S-V-DO
8. Bill tore his pajamas.
   S-V-DO
9. Mr. Bridges was cooking.
   S-V
10. The tunnel was dark.
    S-V-SC
11. The jury has awarded Mr. Hodgkins first prize in the oil painting category.
    S-V-IO-DO
12. One of the speakers called the king a fink.
    S-V-DO-OC
13. The volcano erupted violently.
    S-V
14. The rainy weather made hiking a messy affair.
    S-V-DO-OC
15. The firm promoted John last year.
    S-V-DO

16. Chris cooked us some wonderful crepes last night.
    S-V-IO-DO
17. Many of the sailors went mad.
    S-V-SC
18. The weather had brightened up by the next day.
    S-V
19. Jane found Rupert a delightful companion. (2)
    S-V-IO-DO; S-V-DO-OC
20. Mr. O'Herlihy left his wife a total wreck. (2)
    S-V-IO-DO; S-V-DO-OC

Notice that [20] has a third meaning: that O'Herlihy was a total wreck when he left his wife. The sentence patterns 1–5 do not allow for this interpretation (it would be S-V-DO-SC) because it is rare and is a possibility only for a very small number of verbs, primarily **to leave.** *All three sentence patterns involving* **to leave** *are exemplified in*

   a. Some hikers had left the gate open (S-V-DO-OC)
   b. He left his heirs a tidy fortune (S-V-IO-DO)
   c. She left the meeting angry (S-V-DO-SC)

Exercise 5.4

Which of the following sentences are transitive? For those that are, identify (underline or write out) the noun phrase that is the direct object of the transitive verb. Make sure that you identify the entire direct object and only the direct object!

1. Julie has copied all my linguistics files onto her hard drive.
2. Mr. Dranek looked at me as if I came from another planet.
3. The guys from Red Alert were snoozing in the bottom of the boat.
4. The survivors had improvised a fuel tank out of an old gas can.
5. We examined each box carefully.
6. Day care centers look after the children of the employees.
7. The voters elect a new president every eight years.
8. The groom smoked incessantly.
9. Max was cooking up one of his special breakfasts.
10. The crew from Sweeps Clean was pulling into the driveway.

Sentences (1), (4), (5), (7), and (9) are transitive. The direct objects are:
   1. all my linguistics files

4. *a fuel tank*
5. *each box*
7. *a new president*
9. *one of his special breakfasts*

Exercise 5.5

Adverbials, unlike adverbial complements, can be moved to the front of the sentence or omitted without changing the verb's meaning. Adverbial complements *complete* the sense of the verb; they are often found after verbs in which movement in a direction is involved, and with verbs that easily combine with prepositional phrases. Using these criteria, determine whether the final noun phrase or prepositional phrase in the following sentences is an adverbial or an adverbial complement (these are the only two possibilities in this set of sentences). Always assume the most natural and least forced interpretation of the sentence.

1. Bernadette dropped a quarter in the wishing well.
2. Billy took his medicine in the bathroom.
3. Billy took his medicine into the bathroom.
4. Brutus and his gang attacked Caesar in the Forum.
5. Cassius stabbed Caesar in the chest.
6. Mr. Whitfield spilled his coffee on the rug.
·7. The younger children were playing Monopoly on the rug.
8. A telegram arrived for you during the night.
9. Mr. Harris always receives his guests in the living room.
10. Ms. Thurman invited her friends to a sumptuous party.

Sentences (2), (4), (7), (8) contain adverbials. The remainder have adverbial complements.

Exercise 5.6

In the following sentences, all of which are intransitive, identify any that have understood objects.

1. We listened carefully.
2. Ms. Higgins cooks for twelve people every day.
3. The maharajah died in his sleep that night.
4. Harvey had to fetch and carry for the new office manager.
5. The beans have to soak for four hours.

6. You wash and I'll dry.

7. The water was already boiling.

8. The children were sleeping.

9. In my opinion, he drinks excessively.

10. After the game, Jenny showered and changed.

(2), (4), (6), (9), and (10) (changed) have understood objects.

Exercise 5.7

Indirect objects and direct objects refer to different entities (things and people); direct objects and object complements refer to the same entity. Using this criterion of same/different reference, identify the IO-DO sentences and the DO-OC ones.

1. Marlys was telling the children a ghost story.
   IO-DO

2. They elected Mr. Fitzpatrick recorder of deeds for the county.
   DO-OC

3. The chamber of commerce has declared Betsylou Strawberry Queen of Berkshire County.
   DO-OC

4. The Duchess threw Alice a pink flamingo.
   IO-DO

5. Jack and Mo are cooking the orphans a wonderful breakfast.
   IO-DO

6. We have named Siegmund chair of the Pollution Committee.
   DO-OC

7. Someone has sold Mr. Braithwaite a used mandolin.
   IO-DO

8. The local citizens called our quarter of town "Little Italy."
   DO-OC

9. Janet poured old Miss Madder a stiff vodka.
   IO-DO

10. Mattie sent the dean of Arts and Sciences a box of chocolates.
    IO-DO

Exercise 5.9

This question practices the recent discussion of diagramming and reviews the earlier material in Chapter 2.

In the following abstract diagrams, the nodes in (1) and (2) are labeled with meaningless letters. In (3), the underline labels are equally meaningless colors. Answer the questions beside each diagram with T or F:

1.

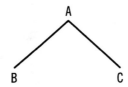

  i. A dominates B. ___T___
  ii. C and B exhaustively dominate A.___F___
  iii. A immediately dominates B and C. ___T___
  iv. A is a branching node.___T___

2.

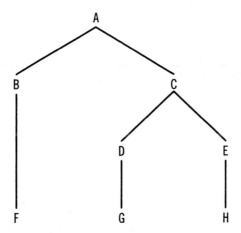

  i. F, G, and H together are a phrase. ___T___
  ii. A dominates E and F. ___T___
  iii. G and H are exhaustively dominated by C. ___T___
  iv. F and G together are a phrase. ___F___
  v. B is a branching node. ___F___

3.

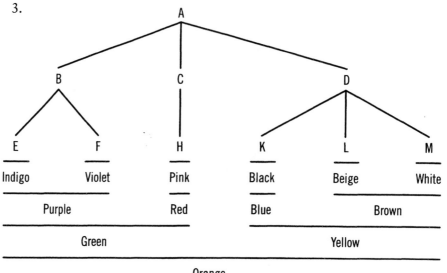

i. Brown is a phrase. ___*F*___

ii. A immediately dominates H. ___*F*___

iii. Yellow is a phrase. ___*T*___

iv. B functions as a Purple.___*T*___

v. K, L, and M are a D functioning as a Yellow.___*T*___

vi. Brown is a D. ___*F*___

vii. A exhaustively dominates E, F, K, L, and M. ___*F*___

viii. Green is a phrase. ___*F*___

ix. D immediately and exhaustively dominates K, L, and M.___*T*___

x. A immediately dominates C and D.___*T*___

Exercise 5.10

Diagram sentences 2, 8, and 9 in Exercise 5.7. Use the triangle convention to abbreviate the NPs.

Sentences 2 and 9 are diagrammed as follows:

2. They elected Mr. Fitzpatrick recorder of deeds for the county.

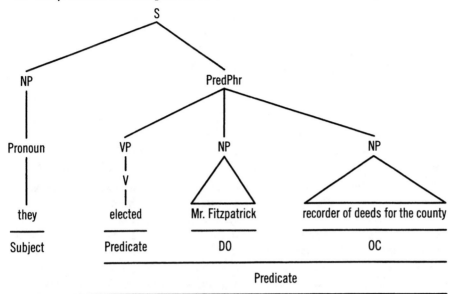

9. Janet poured old Miss Madder a stiff vodka.

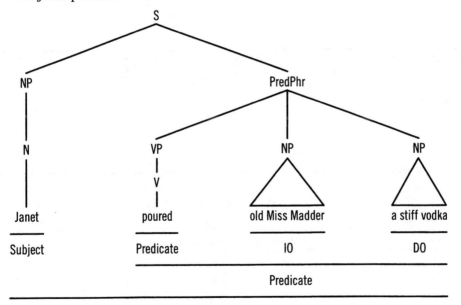

Exercise 5.11

(For class discussion) The principle that the indirect object is a human recipient does not always hold up. Obviously, we use the names of domestic animals as indirect objects (as in *It's time to give Fido his dinner*). But there are also expressions like

1. They gave the wall a coat of paint
2. The player gave the football a kick

Can you think of other kinds of examples in which the indirect object is not the recipient of a transfer? How do sentences like (1) and (2) differ from other kinds of sentences with indirect objects? What kinds of verbs occur in them?

*(1) The verb is always **give**. There are no alternatives using verbs like **hand over** or **present**. (2) The predicate phrase may have the same meaning as one of the nouns, such as **paint** or **kick**; often, this noun can be used as the main verb with very little change in meaning (**to paint, to kick**). Unlike the normal sense of **to give**, which means merely to transfer an object or idea into the possession of the recipient, **to give** here implies an **effect** of some kind on the receiver of the action. Other examples: **gave the baby a bath, gave her friend a funny look, gave him a shove** (**poke, push, jab,** and so on), **gave him a scolding, gave the car a final polish**. Gestures such as **gave me the thumbs-up** (**a shrug, a grin, a nod, the finger,** and others) also belong here.*

EXERCISE ANSWERS: CHAPTER 6

Exercise 6.1

Display the base form, *-ing* form, *-en* form, general present, *-s* present, and past tense of the following verbs (indicate any alternative forms you can think of): go, bear, (to) fell (a tree), buy, shine, strive, speed, lay, spit, hang, creep, steal, let, fall, set, think, bring, beat, speak, run, lie, strike, get, dare, tear.
Sample answers:

Base form	*-ing* Form	*-en* Form	General present	*-s* Present	Past tense
go	going	gone	go	goes	went
fell	felling	felled	fell	fells	felled
think	thinking	thought	think	thinks	thought
shine	shining	shone/shined	shine	shines	shone/shined
beat	beating	beaten	beat	beats	beat
strive	striving	striven	strive	strives	strove

Exercise 6.2

Identify the -ing form in each of the following sentences as progressive aspect, modifier, or gerund.

1. John is calling his psychiatrist right now.
2. Anyone wanting to ride The Monster must line up in front of the post.
3. The practice of branding cattle is very cruel.
4. Your son and his friends were plagiarizing term papers.
5. Plagiarizing term papers is a serious offence.
6. Students plagiarizing term papers are always expelled.
7. His career as a wine taster was ruined by his drinking.
8. Fires were already burning when we arrived.
9. Getting up at 6 was an ordeal for Mr. Simmons.
10. Passengers leaving the train were overcome by the fumes.

(1) progressive, (2) modifier, (3) gerund, (4) progressive, (5) gerund, (6) modifier, (7) gerund, (8) progressive, (9) gerund, (10) modifier

Exercise 6.3

(For class discussion) What changes would you want to make in the following sentences, and why?

1. We have arrived in Chicago at 8:41 p.m.

   The perfect aspect is generally not used with exact time expressions.

2. While Jane drank coffee in the lounge, an announcement was suddenly coming over the loudspeakers.

   *The announcement is foregrounded, while Jane's drinking coffee is backgrounded. So the aspects are the wrong way around. The sentence would sound better if the aspects were reversed: While Jane **was drinking** coffee in the lounge, an announcement suddenly **came** . . .*

3. Last night you can see the Northern Lights from our bedroom window.

   *The present-tense **can** is incompatible with the past-tense adverbial **last night**.*

4. Senator Frogworthy has lain a wreath at the Soldiers' Memorial.

   *The -en form of the transitive verb to lay is not **lain** but **laid**.*

5. I might could replace the spark plugs.

   ***Might could**, a so-called double modal construction, is heard in some regional dialects, but should be avoided in formal writing. Use instead: **might be able to**.*

6. Mario hitted the puck behind the Penguins' own goal.

   The past tense of to hit is simply hit.

7. Those strange creatures have abducting my mother-in-law.

   The perfect auxiliary have must be followed by the -en form, not the -ing form, of the verb

8. Someone have must taken money from the Rwandan Relief box.

   The order of auxiliaries in the verb phrase is Modal + Perfect: must have, not have must.

9. Silvester wanted to try and rescue the mountaineers.

   In formal writing, try and should be replaced by try to.

10. Nervously, Harvey rung Dr. Tuggem's doorbell.

    The past tense of to ring is rang. Rung is the -en form. (Rung is, however, often used in speech as the past tense and is gaining ground in the written language.)

11. Help me—I shall drown!

    Shall is moribund in both written and spoken English. It suggests a strong resolve or obligation, and so here it sounds especially strange. Replacement: "I'm drowning!"

12. The loss of weight in a body immersed in a fluid is equaling the weight of fluid it displaces.

    General truths like this one need the present tense rather than the progressive: replace is equaling with equals.

13. Mr. Silliman often uses to wish he could be a clown.

    Used to occurs only in the past tense. Its present-tense equivalent is simply the general or -s present: often wishes.

14. We require that you are prepared to leave on 24 hours' notice.

    In formal written English the subjunctive is still required in sentences like this. Correct: that you be prepared to leave.

15. Now that you have explained your actions, you can leave.

    The use of may rather than can in the permission sense is still preferred in formal contexts.

Exercise 6.4

Convert the present tenses into the past tense. Note in doing this exercise that you must be careful not to change any parts of the sentence other than the tense.

Example:

The city council is going to discuss the new stadium
-> The city council was going to discuss the new stadium.

That is, "is going to discuss" should not be changed to "discussed," "will discuss," or the like, but only to "*was* going to discuss."

1. The bus must come to a complete stop at every railroad crossing.

    *The bus **had to** come to a complete stop at every railroad crossing.*

2. He says he will make an appointment with his therapist.

    *He **said** he **would** make an appointment with his therapist.*

3. Dr. Nincombe-Poope is supposed to have been checking up on the inmates.

    *Dr. Nincombe-Poope **was** supposed to have been checking up on the inmates.*

4. Someone has been putting salt water in the ice trays.

    *Someone **had** been putting salt water in the ice trays.*

5. Hennypenny lays two eggs every day.

    *Hennypenny **laid** or **used to lay** two eggs every day.*

6. Every year the Youngstown Twisters beat the Louisville Loopers in the regional frisbee tournament.

    *Every year the Youngstown Twisters **beat** or **used to beat** the Louisville Loopers in the regional frisbee tournament.*

7. The graduate students lie around on the beach all weekend.

    *The graduate students **lay** or **used to lie** around on the beach all weekend.*

8. Marvin pleads guilty to the piracy charge.

    *Marvin **pleaded** or **pled guilty** to the piracy charge.*

9. The Martians are watching us through their telescopes.

    *The Martians **were** watching us through their telescopes.*

10. The students at that college have to attend church services every morning.

    *The students at that college **had** to attend church services every morning.*

Exercise 6.5

Diagram the following sentences. See the appendix to this chapter for specimen diagrams and guidelines on diagramming elements of the verb phrase.

1. Last Sunday, Sebastian may have been playing the tuba.

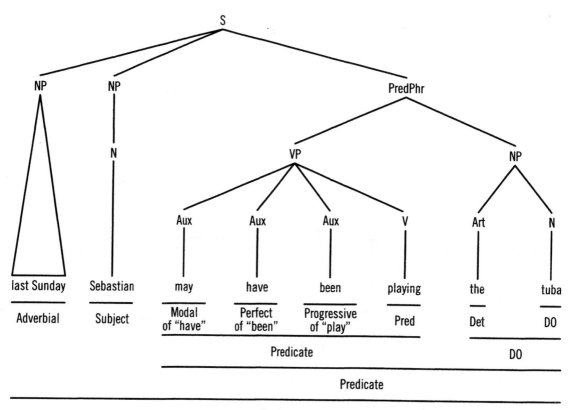

2. Explosions have been rocking the town since early morning.

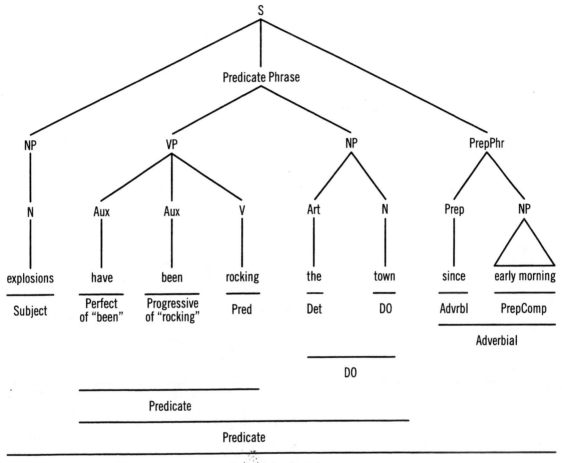

Exercise 7.1

Draw form-function diagrams of the following noun phrases. Assume that the NP is within a sentence and that it is the direct object.

Sample diagrams of (6) and (7). The diagrams assume that in (6) **with the smallest population in the country** *modifies* **state**, *and in (7)* **with its impressive skyscrapers** *modifies* **capital**.

6. the capital of the state with the smallest population in the country

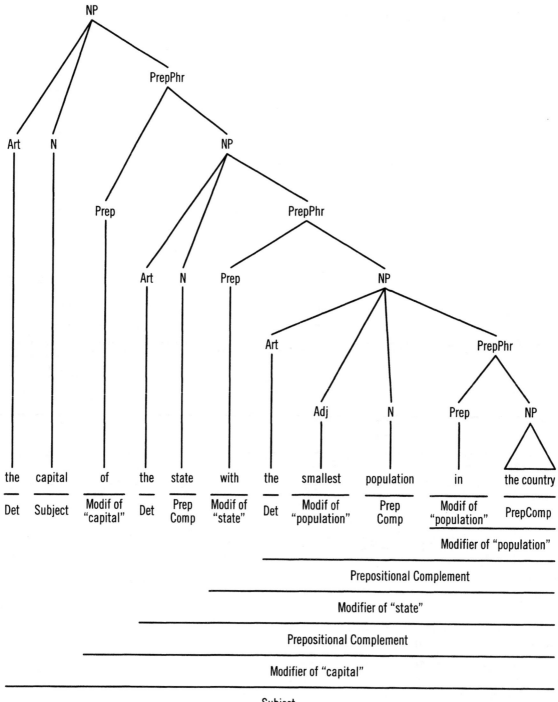

7. the capital of the state with its impressive skyscrapers

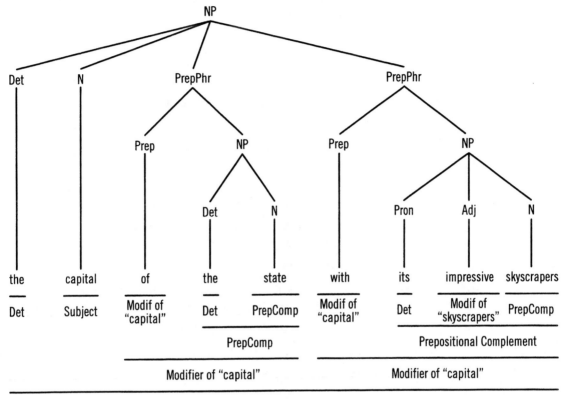

Exercise 7.2

Describe, on the basis of the following sentences, the principle for deciding whether to write *on+to, up+on,* and *in+to* as unit words or as two separate words. Use the grammatical concepts that have been taught in this book, including diagramming.

1. We sent the letter on to my parents.
2. They poured concrete onto the tiles.
3. Someone turned Lefty in to the FBI.
4. Mario turned Princess Jacinta into a frog.
5. The roof rested upon stately columns.
6. The construction workers were resting up on the patio.

The prepositions are written separately if they are parts of different phrases, as in (1), (3), and (6). They are written together if they form a single compound preposition that is part of the same prepositional phrase, as in (2),

*(4), and (5). Diagrams would show **sent the letter on** in (1) to be a transitive phrasal verb construction, with **to my parents** as an adverbial complement; and **onto the tiles** in (2) to be a prepositional phrase functioning as an adverbial complement of **poured**, with the preposition **onto** followed by the prepositional complement **the tiles**.*

Exercise 7.3

Identify sentences that have adverbial complements and sentences that have postcore phrases.

1. She was lecturing to a hundred students.
2. He exchanged his Volvo for a Ford.
3. Rollo has had nothing to eat since Saturday.
4. Hans directed his question to the pompous officials.
5. Ms. Jackson was a stubborn woman, in my opinion.
6. They played "Rudolf the Red-Nosed Reindeer" to the delighted children.
7. The fiesta lasted until midnight.
8. The group played country and western music until midnight.
9. Al drove a truck for many years.
10. They built a neat little treehouse in their backyard.

Adverbial complements: (1), (2), (4), (6), (7)

Postcore phrases: (3), (5), (8), (9), (10)

Exercise 7.4

(For class discussion) What changes would you want to make in the following sentences, and why?

1. We complimented the twins about their pretty dresses.

   *The verb **to compliment** is a prepositional verb, and its accompanying preposition is **on**, not **about**.*
2. At page ninety-six John opened the book.

   At page ninety-six is an adverbial complement and cannot normally precede the subject.
3. Two teenaged boys were watching the younger members of the family over.

   ***Watch over** is not a phrasal verb but a prepositional verb. Therefore the preposition cannot follow the direct object.*
4. You will be borrowing always money from them.

*The error here is in the placement of the adverb **always**, which must be put inside the verb phrase, usually after the first auxiliary (**you will always be borrowing**). **Always** shares this positional feature with a number of other shorter adverbs.*

5. Someone had filled up it.

   *The preposition in a phrasal verb cannot be placed after the direct object if the direct object is a pronoun. Change **filled up it** to **filled it up**.*

6. They sold rich financiers off their estate.

   *Indirect objects are at least awkward with phrasal verbs, and this is especially so if the indirect object is a lexical noun rather than a pronoun. Better: **sold their estate off to rich financiers**.*

7. We moved the dynamite farther away the fire.

   ***Away** is not a preposition but an adverb, so the sentence is a preposition short. Correct: **away from the fire**.*

8. With hamburgers and french fries they plied those little brats.

   ***With hamburgers and french fries** is an adverbial complement of the prepositional verb **to ply**. It may not come at the start of the sentence. Change to: **We plied those little brats with hamburgers and french fries**.*

9. We are looking greatly forward to your party next week.

   *The rules for the placement of adverbials in English are quite complex, and not all of them could be discussed in this book. Prepositional phrase adverbials are especially limited in where they can go. One place where prepositional phrases do not commonly occur is within a phrasal verb between the verb and the preposition. So the two words **look forward** can't be separated by a prepositional phrase.*

10. The judge confined to the matter of the trust fund.

    ***To confine** is a transitive-only verb and must have a direct object NP such as **her remarks**.*

Exercise 7.5

Sentences to diagram.

Because of space limitations, some of the complex diagrams are given in fragments.

1. John lost touch with the friends of his roommate.

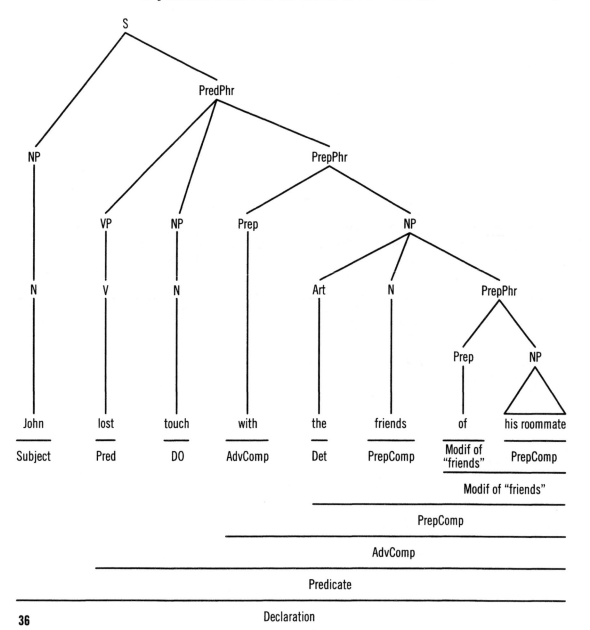

Declaration

2. You should look in on Ms. Bills on your way to the school. *Partial diagram (subject missing)*

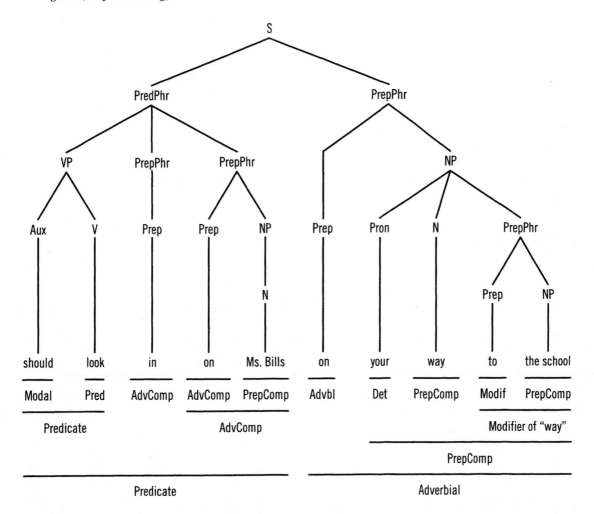

3. I would put his success down to hard work in the design phase of the project by the Red Team. *Partial diagram (major adverbial complement only)*

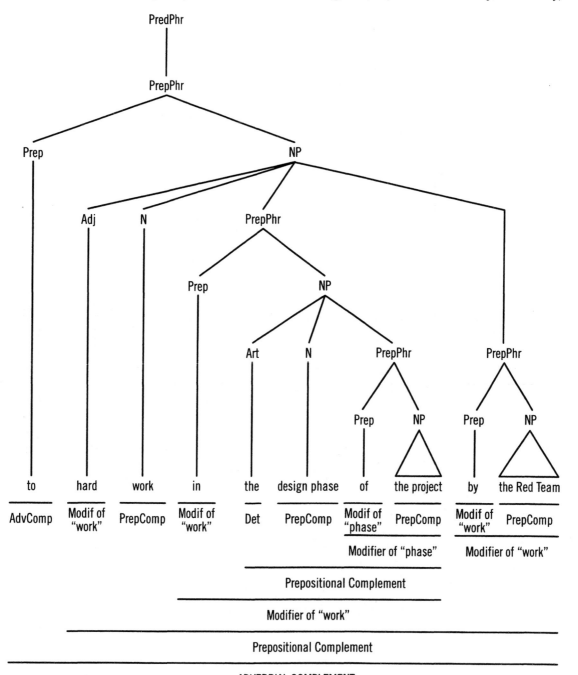

*(I is subject; **would put** is a verb phrase consisting of the aux/modal **would** and the verb **put**; **his success** is the direct object of **put**; **down** is a prepositional phrase functioning as an adverbial complement of **put**.)*

Exercise 7.6

Choosing from the list of words provided, create two grammatical sentences of each of the seven basic sentence patterns; vary the words as much as possible. The sentence patterns are repeated here for your convenience:

1. S-V
2. S-V-SC
3. S-V-DO
4. S-V-IO-DO
5. S-V-DO-OC
6. S-V-AdvComp
7. S-V-DO-AdvComp

   Determiners: *the, a, this, that, some*

   Nouns: *prince, dragon, wizard, cave, ring, dungeon*

   Verbs: *carried, escaped, gave, turned, seemed, made, fainted, handed, considered, ran*

   Adjectives: *frightened, fierce, angry, scary, clever*

   Prepositions: *with, into, from*

   Example sentences:

1. *S-V: This wizard escaped*
2. *S-V-SC: The dragon seemed frightened*
3. *S-V-DO: Some prince made this ring*
4. *S-V-IO-DO: The wizard handed that prince a ring*
5. *S-V-DO-OC: The prince considered the wizard scary*
6. *S-V-AdvComp: The dragon turned into a prince*
7. *S-V-DO-AdvComp: The prince carried the dragon into a dungeon*

Exercise 7.7

Which of the following sentences contain phrasal verbs?

1. Our new Volkswagen could turn on a dime.
2. Partisans had blown up all the bridges.
3. We touched down at exactly 7:23 a.m.
4. Patti insisted on the champagne.

5. The new provost has already turned in his resignation.
6. A cold wind was blowing up the narrow canyon.
7. A member of the audience was reading off every name on the program in a loud whisper.
8. His recklessness with facts would have made his old professor turn in his grave.
9. None of the adults knew how to turn on the VCR.
10. One of the gang showed up next day with a bouquet of flowers.

The following sentences contain phrasal verbs: (2), (3), (5), (7), (9), (10).

Exercise 7.8

Find, in the following sentences, examples of prepositional phrases with an NP; prepositional phrases without an NP; prepositional phrases modifying a noun; prepositional phrases functioning as adverbials; adverbial complements other than phrasal verbs; phrasal verbs; prepositional verbs. (Of course there may be more than one of these in the same sentence.)

1. Over the years Harvey has simply lost touch with all his old college friends.
2. He could not keep up with his correspondence.
3. Dr. Strange was absentmindedly tapping his pipe on the radiator.
4. At the end of the driveway to the house we could just see Blakeslee's station wagon.
5. He trod down hard on the gas pedal at the first corner.
6. Fred looked "hypocrite" up in *Webster's Third*.
7. Despite our fears, Julius pulled through.
8. The schooner was slowly making headway against a fierce northeasterly gale.
9. The other members of the team looked up to Janice.
10. I referred them to Eisenblut's classic study of gerbils.

Prepositional phrases with NP:
1. *over the years, with all his old college friends*
2. *with his correspondence*
3. *on the radiator*
4. *at the end of the driveway to the house, of the driveway to the house, to the house*
5. *on the gas pedal, at the first corner*
6. *in* Webster's Third
7. *despite our fears*

8. *against a fierce northeasterly gale*

9. *of the team, to Janice*

10. *to Eisenblut's classic study of gerbils, of gerbils*

Prepositional phrases without an NP:

2. *up*

5. *down*

6. *up*

7. *through*

9. *up*

Prepositional phrases modifying a noun:

4. *of the driveway to the house, to the house*

10. *of gerbils*

Prepositional phrases functioning as adverbials:

1. *Over the years*

4. *At the end of the driveway to the house*

5. *at the first corner*

7. *Despite our fears*

Adverbial complements (other than phrasal verbs):

1. *with all his old college friends*

2. *with his correspondence*

3. *on the radiator*

5. *on the gas pedal*

6. *in* Webster's Third

8. *against a fierce northeasterly gale*

9. *to Janice*

10. *to Eisenblut's classic study of gerbils*

Phrasal verbs:

2. *keep up*

5. *trod down*

6. *looked . . . up*

7. *pulled through*

9. *looked up*

Prepositional verbs:

1. *lost touch with*

2. *keep up with*

5. *trod down on*

6. *looked . . . up in*
8. *was making headway against*
9. *looked up to*
10. *referred them to*

EXERCISE ANSWERS: CHAPTER 8

Exercise 8.1

Change the following sentences by converting the italicized forms into pronouns with the person indicated.

1. *I* have always imagined *myself* to be easygoing. (third-person singular feminine)

   She has always imagined herself to be easygoing.

2. The assistant principal took *hers* away from *her*. (first-person singular)

   The assistant principal took mine away from me.

3. The only person in the room at that time was *you*. (third-person singular masculine)

   The only person in the room at that time was him.

4. *I myself* made this soup from *my* own recipe. (second-person singular)

   You yourself made this soup from your own recipe.

5. The judges will grant *you* an extension. (third-person singular feminine)

   The judges will grant her an extension.

6. *You yourself* stated this in *your* own report. (first-person plural)

   We ourselves stated this in our own report.

7. *She* surprised *herself* with *her* own boldness. (first-person singular)

   I surprised myself with my own boldness.

8. *You* could go off on *your* vacation by *yourself*. (indefinite pronoun "one")

   One could go off on one's vacation by oneself.

9. The scientist must consider the data *the scientist* has gathered before *the scientist* commits *the scientist* to an explicit hypothesis. (third-person singular feminine)

   The scientist must consider the data she has gathered before she commits herself to an explicit hypothesis.

10. A poet must plunge *a poet* deeply into personal experience before *a poet*

can make that experience part of *a poet's.* (third-person singular masculine)

A poet must plunge himself deeply into personal experience before he can make that experience part of his own.

Exercise 8.2

Substitute a single pronoun for the italicized word or phrase. If there is more than one possibility, so state; assume, however, that identical names refer to the same person.

1. Lefty and Marvin slapped *Marvin and Lefty* on the back.

   Lefty and Marvin slapped one another on the back.

2. Jenny Roth indulged *Jenny Roth* in some more peanut brittle.

   Jenny Roth indulged herself in some more peanut brittle.

3. Mitch Funai had already eaten *Mitch Funai's.*

   Mitch Funai had already eaten his.

4. Skippy invited *Skippy's* Mom and Dad into *Skippy's* treehouse.

   Skippy invited her Mom and Dad into her treehouse.

5. *A person* must always pay careful attention to *a person's* grammar when writing *a person's* résumé.

   You (or one) must always pay careful attention to your (or one's) grammar when writing your (or one's) résumé.

6. Nancy had lost *Nancy's* on the subway.

   Nancy had lost hers on the subway.

7. Mike and Susan, *Mike and Susan* must behave *Mike and Susan* while I am away.

   Mike and Susan, you must behave yourselves while I am away.

8. Bill and Emma sold *Bill and Emma's* car, and Grenville and I sold *mine and Grenville's* too.

   Bill and Emma sold their car, and Grenville and I sold ours too.

9. You and your husband can earn *you and your husband* some extra money.

   You and your husband can earn yourselves some extra money.

10. The lieutenant showed Lucy and Verona an old photograph of *me, Verona, and Lucy.*

    The lieutenant showed Lucy and Verona an old photograph of us.

Exercise 8.3

Analyze the italicized NPs in terms of the determiner phrase that determines the head noun. Specifically: Identify the head of the determiner phrase. Identify any pre- and post-determiners and any links (*of*). Be sure to distinguish between the elements of the determiner phrase and any adjectives that might precede the head noun.

1. Bill was going to collect *his new eyeglasses*.

   his is a central determiner; new is an adjective

2. *All of the first thirty eager competitors* received Pittsburgh Marathon T-shirts.

   all is a pre-determiner; of is a link; the is a central determiner; first is a post-determiner; thirty is a post-determiner; eager is an adjective

3. They had an expanded retirement package for *all those fifty-nine former employees*.

   all is a pre-determiner; of is a link; those is a central determiner; fifty-nine is a post-determiner; former is an adjective

4. *A lot of those twenty-three million undecided voters* will be interested in a third party.

   a lot is a pre-determiner; of is a link; those is a central determiner; twenty-three million is a post-determiner; undecided is an adjective

5. *Some of my many friends* sent me birthday cards.

   some is a pre-determiner; of is a link; my is a central determiner; many is a post-determiner

6. *His entire collection of ancient coins* was put up for sale.

   his is a central determiner; entire is an adjective; of ancient coins is a prepositional phrase modifying collection

7. This compromise will alienate *all of their few supporters*.

   all is a pre-determiner; of is a link; their is a central determiner; few is a post-determiner

8. The mayor gave a red rose to *each of the proud veterans*.

   each is a pre-determiner; of is a link; the is a central determiner; proud is an adjective

9. *Several of the attorneys* left on the next train.

   several is a pre-determiner; of is a link; the is a central determiner

10. *None of these twelve upright citizens* will vote for acquittal.

    none is a pre-determiner; of is a link; these is a central determiner; twelve is a post-determiner; upright is an adjective

Exercise 8.4

Fill in the blank with the appropriate form (-s present or general present) of the verb.

1. The new criteria for defining a controlled substance _____ for a change in our enforcement policy. (call)

2. A coven of witches ___ to the air on Halloween. (take)

3. The strange phenomena in the sky ____ attracted the attention of a bright young astronomer. (have)

4. The agenda ___ Mr. Hlubik's promotion. (include)

5. Gymnastics ____ the only sport at which she excels. (be)

6. The newly invented automata ___ the chips to the exact place on the motherboard. (attach)

7. The wealthy alumna ___ donated money for the equipment. (have)

8. The corrigenda ___ to be added to the end of the proofs. (be)

9. A large number of voters ___ troubled by the rising unemployment rate. (be)

10. Every one of Bill's children _____ graduated from college. (have)

(1) call, (2) takes, (3) have, (4) includes, (5) is, (6) attach, (7) has, (8) are, (9) are, (10) has

Exercise 8.5

Identify the italicized nouns as mass or count, and as abstract or concrete.

1. Marsha felt a sharp *pain* in her upper arm as the medic inserted the needle.

2. Someone threw the *basketball* directly at the dean of arts and sciences.

3. The old law resulted in numerous *injustices*.

4. The barbell was made of *steel*.

5. In the courtyard some boys were playing a raucous game of *basketball*.

6. The children got mugs of steaming hot *chocolate*.

7. One of the police used a vulgar *expression*.

8. Mr. Krepke found the head waiter's *arrogance* disturbing.

9. The full *exploration* of the Antarctic took place in the twentieth century.

10. Lefty handed the *money* to the precinct captain.

(1) count, abstract; (2) count, concrete; (3) count, abstract; (4) mass, concrete; (5) mass, abstract; (6) mass, concrete; (7) count, abstract; (8) mass, abstract; (9) count, abstract; (10) mass, concrete

Exercise 8.6

(For class discussion) What changes would you want to make in the following sentences, and why?

1. We would like you to meet next week with several members of the administration and I.

*Since the pronoun is part of the complement of the preposition **with**, it should be in the objective case form: **several members of the administration and me**.*

2. A number of species on the island has already become extinct.

   *A **number of species** is to be interpreted as a plural NP, and the auxiliary should be **have**. The point here is that **number** is no longer understood as the head of the subject NP, but instead a **number (of)** is now a pre-determiner, and the head of the subject NP is the plural noun **species**.*

3. By this criteria, all club members with children would qualify for a dues reduction.

   *Since **criteria** is plural, the form of the demonstrative required is **these** rather than **this**.*

4. That orchard of apple and peach trees as far as the stone wall is all our's.

   *The independent pronoun **ours** is spelled without the apostrophe.*

5. An efficient receptionist will always keep her address file up to date.

   *Gender stereotyping by occupation should be avoided. Change **her** to **his or her**, or, better, recast the sentence with a plural subject: **receptionists . . . their**.*

6. The Anderson's are putting new siding on their house.

   *The s-plural should not have an apostrophe before it. This applies to family names as well as to other kinds of nouns: **the Andersons**.*

7. A basket of lovely spring flowers were lying on the table.

   ***Basket** is the head noun of the subject NP, not a pre-determiner, so the subject NP is singular and the auxiliary should also be singular: **was lying**.*

8. Mr. Hodges was in charge of the childrens' literature section.

   *The noun **child** does not form its plural in -s, and so the possessive plural has the apostrophe before rather than after the s: **children's**.*

9. We were looking forward to the speech of Mr. Breitman.

   *Human possessors, especially names, preferably take the morphological rather than the periphrastic possessive: **Mr. Breitman's speech**.*

10. The police line was blocking the people's in the front row view of the stage.

    *The possessive marker is placed at the very end of the noun phrase: **the people in the front row's view**.*

Exercise 8.7

Indicate for each of the sentences which **some** is intended; the one for the indefinite mass or plural noun, or the one for the singular count noun.

1. Some idiot with diplomatic license plates has parked their car in our driveway.
2. Some water had leaked into the gas line.
3. That was some whale we saw out in the channel.
4. Oliver asked for some more of the delicious soup.
5. Some paint was on the car and some on the driveway.
6. Mattie had to go to the hardware store and get some nails.
7. Somehow some arsenic had found its way into the fondue.
8. Jim had gone to Acapulco with some woman he had met in Los Angeles.
9. Some quick-thinking bystanders grabbed the child.
10. That idiot Podgieter has deleted all my messages—some "facilitator" he has turned out to be!

(1) singular count noun, (2) indefinite mass noun, (3) singular count noun, (4) indefinite mass noun, (5) indefinite mass noun, (6) indefinite mass noun, (7) indefinite mass noun, (8) singular count noun, (9) indefinite mass noun, (10) singular count noun

EXERCISE ANSWERS: CHAPTER 9

Exercise 9.1

Diagram the following NPs as subjects. Assume the most natural interpretation of the NP. If you nonetheless feel the phrase could with about equal likelihood be understood two ways, diagram it both ways.

Sample diagrams for (1), (2), and (5)

1. the complex motor vehicle regulations

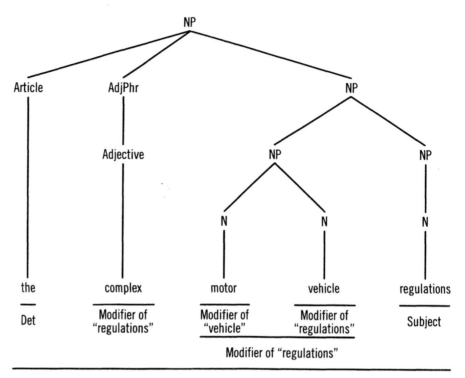

2. some quietly reading library users

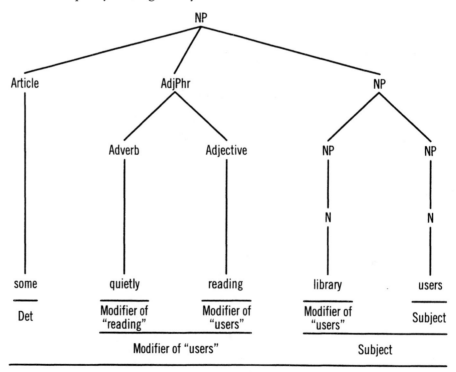

4. a very badly frightened babysitter

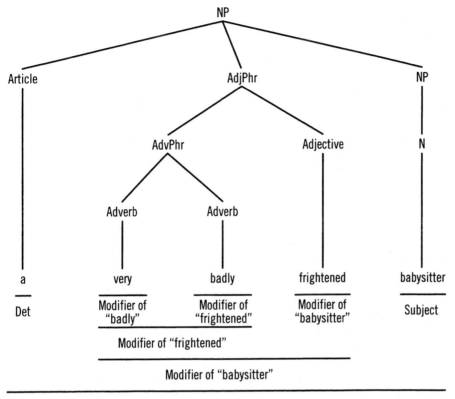

Exercise 9.2

Identify any adjective phrases that contain adjectival complements.

1. They made the essay subject to strict length limits.
    subject to strict length limits
2. Their attempt to open the door was successful on the third try.
    (No adjective complement)
3. The children were afraid of the strange creature in the closet.
    afraid of the strange creature in the closet
4. Alphonse appeared unwilling to write the letter.
    unwilling to write the letter
5. They gave a new essay subject to the students.
    (No adjective complement)

6. Gregory is good at chess.

   good at chess

7. The spooky story made the children glad for their warm, secure beds.

   glad for their warm, secure beds

8. The rest of the class went green with envy over Marsha's score.

   green with envy over Marsha's score

9. We quickly became exasperated at the staff's incompetence.

   exasperated at the staff's incompetence

10. They found that Schreiber was quick to anger and slow to forgive.

    quick to anger, slow to forgive

Exercise 9.3

(For discussion or group work) Fill out the table by checking adjectives that are

(A) only attributive

(B) only predicative

(C) used either attributively or predicatively but with somewhat different meanings

(D) able to take a complement

(E) used only with a complement

Some of the assignments made in the following table may need further discussion, and there will not be complete agreement.

		A	B	C	D	E
(1)	main		X			
(2)	erroneous	X				
(3)	utter		X			
(4)	comfortable	X				
(5)	fond					X
(6)	tantamount			X		
(7)	latest				X	
(8)	very		X			
(9)	glad					X
(10)	chief		X			
(11)	enough					X
(12)	ready					X
(13)	absolute	X				
(14)	amazing					X
(15)	able					X
(16)	suicidal	X				
(17)	ancient	X				
(18)	aware			X		
(19)	red					X
(20)	jealous					X

Exercise 9.4

Diagram each of the following three sentences (discussed in 9.4 of the text) two ways to reflect the structural ambiguity.

  1. The engineers have been looking for a problem in the hydraulic system.

Answer:

*The first sentence is diagrammed as follows. The A diagram analyzes the direct object as **a problem in the hydraulic system**, while the B diagram assumes that the direct object is **a problem**, with **in the hydraulic system** understood as the focus of their search (and therefore an adverbial complement of **look**).*

A.

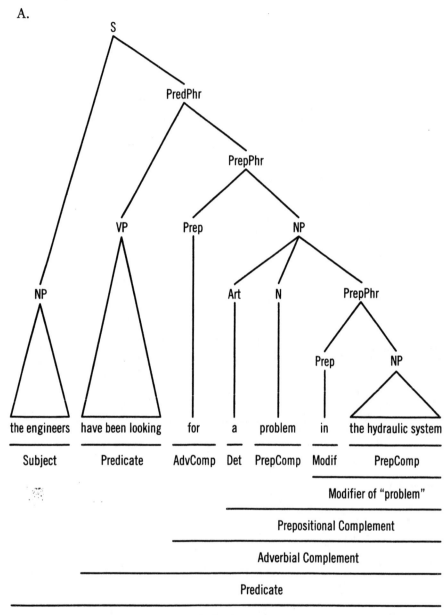

the engineers	have been looking	for	a	problem	in	the hydraulic system
Subject	Predicate	AdvComp	Det	PrepComp	Modif	PrepComp

Modifier of "problem"

Prepositional Complement

Adverbial Complement

Predicate

Declaration

B.

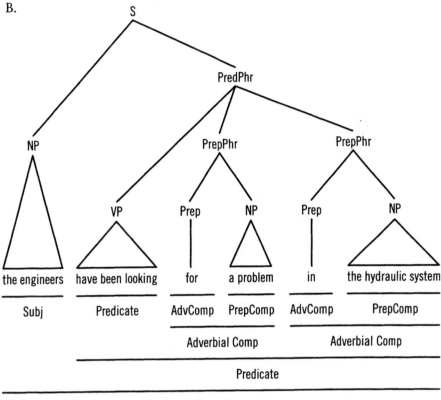

Exercise 9.5

Expand the adjective(s) in these sentences to a comparative, using the NP in parentheses as the standard for the comparison.

1. Ulan Bator is far away. (St. Petersburg)
   Ulan Bator is farther (or further) away than St. Petersburg.
2. A pound of feathers is heavy. (a pound of nails)
   A pound of feathers is heavier than a pound of nails.
3. The wines of the Asti region are bubbly. (champagne)
   The wines of the Asti region are bubblier than champagne.
4. The Newburg *Gazette* is an old, good, and highly regarded journal. (the Oldville *Dispatch*)
   The Newburg Gazette *is an older, better, and more highly regarded journal than the Oldville* Dispatch.

5. A freelance mechanic will often give an honest and straightforward appraisal. (the average employee of a large chain of garages)

   A freelance mechanic will often give a more honest and straightforward (or more straightforward) appraisal than the average employee of a large chain of garages.

6. Dotheboys College is a large, prestigious, and expensive institution. (St. Jasper's)

   Dotheboys College is a larger, more prestigious, and more expensive institution than St. Jasper's.

7. The Nashville Nukes are bad losers. (the Knoxville Niners)

   The Nashville Nukes are worse losers than the Knoxville Niners.

8. Octopus Industries Limited have pursued the merger for a long time and obstinately. (Coordinated Widgets Incorporated)

   Octopus Industries Limited have pursued the merger for a longer time and more obstinately than Coordinated Widgets Incorporated.

9. A pasta and salad diet is healthy, low in cholesterol, and nutritious. (some of the faddish new health foods)

   A pasta and salad diet is healthier, lower in cholesterol, and more nutritious than some of the faddish new health foods.

10. The bond market has performed badly and given holders little return on their investment. (the mutual funds)

    The bond market has performed worse and given holders less return on their investment than the mutual funds.

Exercise 9.6

(For class discussion) What changes would you want to make in the following sentences, and why?

1. We were aware for the finance committee's objections.

   *The adjective **aware** takes a complement with the preposition **of** rather than **for**.*

2. Barbieri's ice cream is more tasty, more costly, and refreshinger than Mozzarelli's.

   *The comparative of the adjective **refreshing** must be periphrastic (**more refreshing**). Tasty and costly, on the other hand, have morphological comparatives **tastier** and **costlier**.*

3. With Hrdlicka's theory, several scientists have independently noted a serious problem.

   *The prepositional phrase **with Hrdlicka's theory** is a modifier of **problem** and cannot be moved out of the NP to the beginning of the sentence.*

4. The first to cross the finish line runner was June Novak.

   *The adjectival phrase **first to cross the finish line** (in which the adjective **first** has a complement **to cross the finish line**) must be placed after the noun it modifies. The phrase is an extended modifier; extended modifiers cannot precede the head noun but must follow it.*

5. With his bonus he bought a quietly and efficiently washing machine.

   *The problem here is with the modifier **washing**, which is not an adjective but a gerund, and therefore a noun,. The adverbs **quietly** and **efficiently** would be appropriate only if the word modifying the noun machine were an adjective.*

6. David did real well in his examinations.

   ***Real** is used almost universally as a modifier of **well** and other adverbs and adjectives in spoken English, but should be avoided in formal writing in favor of **really**.*

7. Attorneys and financial planners will work together for their client to make the largest possible profit.

   *The sentence is ambiguous. The words **for their client to make the largest possible profit** could be either one or two phrases, depending on whether the clients or the lawyers and financial planners will make the profit. Possible rewrites of the sentence would be, depending on which meaning is intended,*

   Attorneys and financial planners will work together so that their client can make the largest possible profit**, or **Attorneys and financial planners will work together for their client so as to make the largest possible profit.

8. We wanted a conference that would be different in significant ways than that of the previous year.

   *Although the use of **than** in the comparative is hardly a serious error, most style books and manuals recommend **from**.*

9. We examined most of the files on the top shelf in my office.

   *Another ambiguity stemming from too many prepositional phrases at the end of the sentence. Is **in my office** the place where the shelf was located or where the examining of the files was done? (A third interpretation, far-fetched but grammatically possible, is that the people examining the files were themselves on the top shelf in my office.)*

10. Because of his tact and good manners, Peter would be the best person to telephone.

    *We don't know whether Peter is the subject or the object of the telephoning. Substitute, as the case may be, **Peter would be the best person to do the telephoning (make the telephone call, etc.)**, or **Peter would be the best person for us (you, etc.) to telephone**.*

EXERCISE ANSWERS: CHAPTER 10

Exercise 10.1

(For class discussion) What changes would you want to make in the following if you were writing formal sentences, and why? (Which of the sentences are possible in spoken dialects or older usage, or in less usual contexts?)

1. We knew not the reason for his anger.

   To know no longer has a negative without an operator such as do; but know not rather than do not know lasted until well into the nineteenth century and may be familiar to you from Shakespeare and older Bible translations. Correct here is: We did not know ...

2. The babysitter does not will come over tonight.

   The modal auxiliaries, such as will, never take do in the negative: will not come over.

3. Few of the guests ate some of the stuffed olives.

   Few being a negative quantifier, some must be replaced by any.

4. All of the board members received any e-mail messages.

   Since the sentence does not contain a negative, any in place of some is not motivated here.

5. The children didn't be good all day.

   The verb to be is the only verb that forms a negative without using an operator such as do.

6. No one has bought no cheese today.

   In any natural interpretation of this sentence, no cheese should be replaced by any cheese. A strained reading could come up with a sense in which every customer bought some cheese.

7. The new highway has not hardly had any effect on the congestion at rush hour.

   While frequently heard in spoken English all over the world, the combination of not and hardly results in a double negative and should be avoided in formal writing.

8. Scarcely the echoes of the explosion had died away when a squad of agents burst in through the front entrance.

   Sentence-initial scarcely requires negative inversion; that is, the next element in the sentence must be an operator: Scarcely had the echoes ...

9. John slept a wink the night before the trial.

   Sleep a wink is an idiom that is used only in the negative, as in didn't sleep a wink.

10. Motorists are forbidden to bring some inflammable items through the tunnel.

   A small number of verbs, including to forbid, are already negative, and follow the some/any rule in requiring some in the predicate to be replaced by any: Motorists are forbidden to bring any inflammable items through the tunnel.

Exercise 10.2

Determine the possible scope of the negation in each sentence. Note any places where more than one scope interpretation is possible.

1. Dr. Skimpitt had not read the report carefully.

   carefully

2. One of the committee members did not approve of the idea.

   approve of the idea

3. Not one of the committee members approved of the idea.

   one

4. The CEO didn't donate a single penny to the Widows' Fund.

   a single penny

5. I don't believe that the IRS cares a fig about your convenience.

   a fig

6. He did not speak very clearly.

   very clearly

7. They had not read all of *War and Peace.*

   all of War and Peace or read all of War and Peace, with slightly different meanings

8. I am not going because she asked me.

   because she asked me or am going

9. Sometimes she does not eat a thing all day.

   eat a thing

10. Johnny Mack Brown did not meet Pancho until the very end of the movie.

   until the very end of the movie

Exercise 10.3

Diagram the following sentences from Exercise 10.2.

   Diagrams of (1) and (2):

1. Dr. Skimpitt had not read the report carefully.

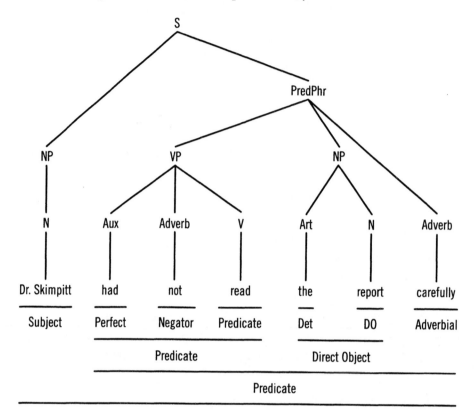

2. One of the committee members did not approve of the idea.

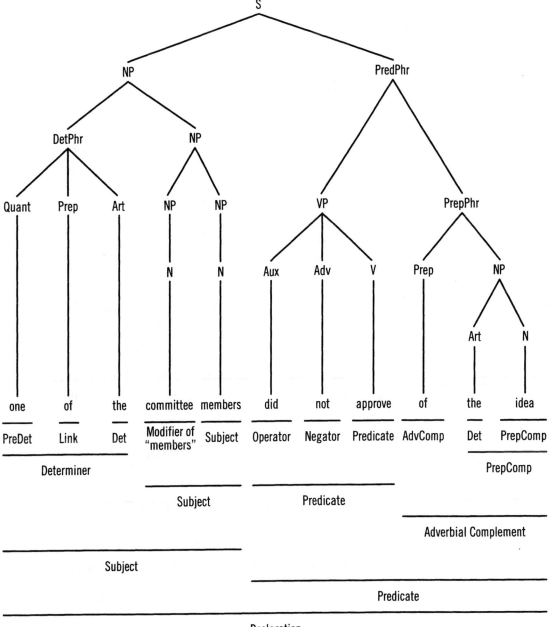

EXERCISE ANSWERS: CHAPTER 11

Exercise 11.1

Convert the following sentences into the passive.

1. The War Office has canceled Franklin's leave.

   Franklin's leave has been canceled by the War Office.

2. The negotiators for the IRS insisted on this guarantee.

   This guarantee was insisted on by the negotiators for the IRS.

3. The attorneys and the board of governors drew up a new agreement.

   A new agreement was drawn up by the attorneys and the board of governors.

4. FBI agents were secretly taping the proceedings.

   The proceedings were secretly being taped by FBI agents.

5. One of the work-study students must have stapled the copies back to front.

   The copies must have been stapled back to front by one of the work-study students.

6. A snowplow has been clearing our street.

   Our street has been cleared by a snowplow.

7. A team from *National Geographic* will be photographing the eruption.

   The eruption will be photographed by a team from National Geographic.

8. Only James Bond can identify the second agent.

   The second agent can only be identified by James Bond (or: can be identified only by James Bond).

9. The mayor offered the protesters a chance to leave quietly.

   A chance to leave quietly was offered the protesters by the mayor.

10. The government attorneys went closely into the question of Rookhurst's dealings with the union leaders.

    The question of Rookhurst's dealings with the union leaders was gone into closely by the government attorneys.

Exercise 11.2

Rewrite, changing the parts in italics from active to passive or vice versa in order to place thematic NPs in the subject position. Delete any of the NPs if this would improve the sentence.

1. Mr. Holthausen was suffering from chest pains, and *medics took him to the hospital.*

   *Mr. Holthausen was suffering from chest pains and **was taken to the hospital by medics.***

2. Fran got up wearily from her armchair and *the front door was closed by her.*

   *Fran got up wearily from her armchair **and closed the front door.***

3. Our street was blocked by snow, but *a municipal plow cleared it before I had to leave for work.*

   *Our street was blocked by snow, **but was cleared by a municipal plow** before I had to leave for work.*

4. The students cannot do the exercise, but *one of the TAs is helping them.*

   *The students cannot do the exercise, but **they are being helped by one of the TAs.***

5. Michelle sautéed the shrimp, stir-fried some fresh vegetables, and put the garlic bread in the oven, while *a bottle of 1991 Mouton Cadet was opened by her boyfriend.*

   *Michelle sautéed the shrimp, stir-fried some fresh vegetables, and put the garlic bread in the oven, **while her boyfriend opened a bottle of 1991 Mouton Cadet.***

6. Prince Gundolf founded a new university, and *schools and hospitals were built by his brother.*

   *Prince Gundolf founded a new university, and **his brother built schools and hospitals.***

7. There was a storm last night, and *their neighbor's toolshed was blown away by one especially strong gust of wind.*

   *There was a storm last night, and **one especially strong gust of wind blew away their neighbor's toolshed.***

8. One of the boxers was badly cut, and so *they stopped the bout in the third round.*

   *One of the boxers was badly cut, and so **the bout was stopped in the third round.***

9. We tried to reach the hospital, but *a fallen tree blocked our way.*

   *We tried to reach the hospital, but **our way was blocked by a fallen tree.***

10. *Plenty of money was paid by me for these tickets* and I intend to see the performance no matter what.

    *I **paid plenty of money for these tickets** and I intend to see the performance no matter what.*

Exercise 11.3

Use the ability to passivize to decide whether the prepositional phrases are adverbial complements or postcore adverbials. (There may be more than one prepositional phrase in the sentence!)

1. Stanley and Livingstone met in the middle of Africa.
   *No passive is possible—**in the middle of Africa** is a postcore adverbial*
2. The faculty did not approve of the appointment.
   *Can be passivized, with **the appointment** as subject*
3. They read from the Book of Job at the funeral service.
   *Can be passivized, with **the Book of Job** as subject*
4. Every citizen was talking about the affair.
   *Can be passivized, with **the affair** as subject*
5. The economic crisis will call for some creative new approaches.
   *Can be passivized, with **some creative new approaches** as subject*
6. Connie was weeping during the funeral service.
   *No passive is possible—**during the funeral service** is a postcore adverbial*
7. The children have been sleeping since yesterday evening.
   *No passive is possible—**since yesterday evening** is a postcore adverbial*
8. Astonished passersby were staring at the notice board.
   *Can be passivized, with **the notice board** as subject*
9. The other motorists were cursing at the slow old Cadillac.
   *Can be passivized, with **the slow old Cadillac** as subject*
10. Several different families have lived in this house.
    *Can be passivized, with **this house** as subject.*

Exercise 11.4

Decide whether the *-en* forms in the following sentences are adjectives or verbs.

1. A number of trees were blown down in the storm.
2. The union members were unperturbed by the actions of the management.
3. The younger undergraduates were rather confused.
4. The site of Troy was discovered in the nineteenth century by German archeologists.
5. Economists were surprised at the price increases.
6. Dr. Gladhand was quite interested in the progress of the project.

7. The gardens of strongly aromatic flowers and herbs are appreciated by the blind residents.

8. All this time the planet Earth was being closely watched by the distant Martians.

9. Professor Skatter's desk was cluttered.

10. Some of these garments are manufactured by companies with headquarters in Asia and Mexico.

*(1) verb; (2) adjective—there is no verb *to unperturb!; (3) adjective, as shown by the intensifier rather; (4) verb; (5) adjective (it would be possible to add very, for example); (6) adjective (with quite); (7) verb; (8) verb; (9) adjective; (10) verb*

EXERCISE ANSWERS: CHAPTER 12

Exercise 12.1

Decide whether the following sentences are *simple* (consist of only one clause), *compound* (consist of coordinated clauses), or *complex* (consist of a main clause and a subordinate clause).

1. Entwhistle can start the barbecue while Crawford mixes the fruit punch. *(complex)*

2. The early settlers would not eat kangaroo meat, and many of them came close to starvation within easy reach of food. *(compound)*

3. Cheryl was balancing a basketball on her head and doing a tap dance in the foyer. *(compound)*

4. After Sheriff Kunitz had delivered the eulogy, the mournful procession made its way back to the town. *(complex)*

5. With the advent of new submarine technology, underwater archeology at hitherto unthinkable depths has become possible. *(simple)*

6. Dr. Martinez together with all the members of the cheerleading team finally boarded the bus. *(simple)*

7. The minuet's popularity declined so much that by 1815 only a few of the older courtiers could still remember how to do it. *(complex)*

8. The patron insisted that the screen should be carved from mahogany. *(complex)*

9. This wood is tough, and the erratic nature of its grain makes it an unusually difficult medium for the carver. *(compound)*

10. The poor provinces could not grow enough rice for their needs, nor would the wealthier provinces give up any of their surplus. *(compound)*

Exercise 12.2

Coordinate the following pairs of sentences with *and, but, either/or,* or *neither/nor,* using ellipsis, passive, and pronouns where good style would require it.

1. Clouds had moved in during the afternoon. By evening a light rain was falling.

   Clouds had moved in during the afternoon, and by evening a light rain was falling.

2. Our car has been stolen. The police have towed our car away.

   Our car has been either stolen or towed away by the police.

3. Their flight was delayed because of the fog. They are stuck in traffic on the way from the airport.

   Either their flight was delayed because of the fog or they are stuck in traffic on their way from the airport.

4. Jake has looked my phone number up. Jake has written my phone number down.

   Jake has looked up and written down my phone number.

5. Tatwina did not inform us of her plans. Tatwina did not finish the report before she left.

   Tatwina did not inform us of her plans, nor did she finish the report before she left.

6. Robert was not only the youngest person to receive a doctorate. The university awarded Robert's thesis a prize.

   Not only was Robert the youngest person to receive a doctorate, but his thesis was awarded a prize by the university.

7. The crew struggled heroically to save the *Mariposa*. By nightfall the Mariposa had foundered in the heavy seas.

   The crew struggled heroically to save the Mariposa, *but by nightfall she had foundered in the heavy seas.*

8. They must have shredded the incriminating documents. They must have burned the incriminating documents.

   They must have shredded or burned the incriminating documents.

9. The security officers did not notice the break-in. The secretaries did not report the missing documents.

   The security officers did not notice the break-in, nor did the secretaries report the missing documents.

10. Kanaka's fantastic story is a pure fabrication. Something very strange happened at the deserted farmhouse last night.

Either Kanaka's fantastic story is a pure fabrication, or something very strange happened at the deserted farm house last night.

Exercise 12.3

Diagram these sentences *without* using the triangle convention.

1. Peter will be invited to the party but will not be introduced to Janine.

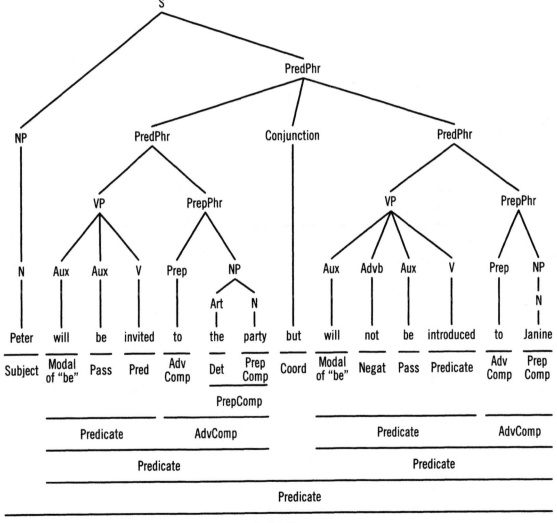

2. The attorneys did not appear, and the judge was very offended.

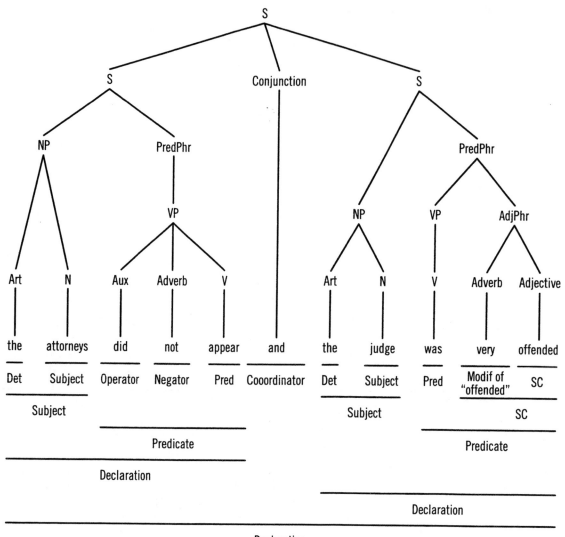

3. The project got Milford interested, but funding was denied by the agency.

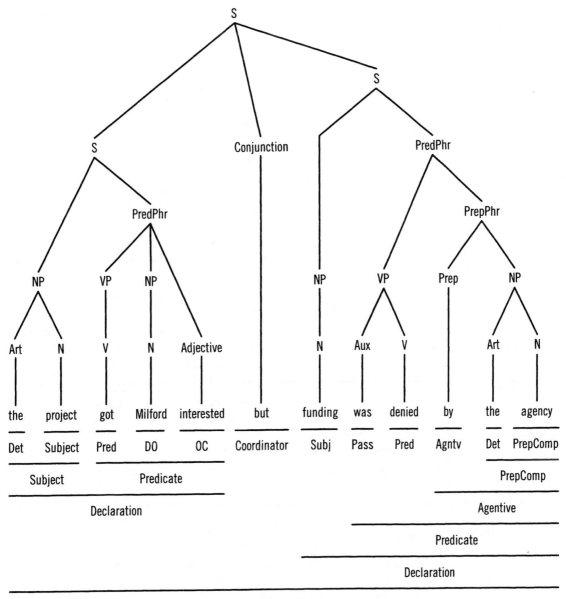

Exercise 12.4

(For class discussion) What changes would you want to make in the following sentences, and why?

1. Our neighbor, not to mention her two children and their dog, are coming over for supper.

    *The verb form **are** points to a plural subject. But the only subject is **our neighbor** (singular). The expression **not to mention** is not a true conjunction and in formal writing doesn't link up with another noun to form a conjoined NP.*

2. By replacing the chief of police, the mayor hopes to strengthen and make the force more efficient.

    *Coordinators must link phrases of the same type. The **and** here links a verb **strengthen** with a predicate phrase **make the force more efficient**, giving rise to two problems: not only are two different phrase types being coordinated, but the verb **strengthen** doesn't have a direct object! One possible change would be: . . . **to strengthen the force and make it more efficient.***

3. The Roman Catholic archbishop, as well as clergy of other faiths, have spoken out against the proposed law.

    *The error here is the same as in (1): **as well as** is not a true conjunction, and cannot create a plural NP. Change **have spoken** to **has spoken**.*

4. They replaced the fenders, the badly dented hood, the cracked wind-shield, and repainted the entire car.

    *Here again, the series of conjoined NPs ends in a different kind of phrase, a predicate phrase **repainted the entire car**. Change the sentence to: **They replaced the fenders, the badly dented hood, and the cracked windshield, and repainted the entire car.***

5. Because of the incessant rain, Vanessa could not play tennis nor the children could go on their picnic.

    *Nor requires negative inversion, that is, it must be followed by an operator: . . . **nor could the children** . . .*

6. Sergei was dissatisfied both with his job and his family life.

    *The position of **both** in **both . . . and** should be before the first of the two phrases being conjoined, here the two NPs **his job and his family life**. Both must therefore come immediately before **his job**: **Sergei was dissatisfied with both his job and his family life.***

7. Cheryl left this cigarette butt under the sofa, or Gregory.

    *Generally, the two phrases being coordinated must be adjacent. Change the subject to **Cheryl or Gregory**.*

8. Sam trimmed the artichoke hearts and marinated.

   The same basic error as in (7), this time with coordinated verbs: Sam trimmed and marinated the artichoke hearts.

9. Either the wheel axles or the chain are slipping.

   The most recent NP controls the verb agreement, in this case the singular NP the chain: Either the wheel axles or the chain is slipping.

10. Davie was nervous about the dispatch slips and questioned by the harbor police.

    Although the element that has been dropped in the second clause is was, it is not the same kind of was as the one in the first clause! The first was is a lexical verb, whereas the second was, the one that has dropped, is the passive auxiliary. Change to: Davie was nervous about the dispatch slips and was questioned by the harbor police.

EXERCISE ANSWERS: CHAPTER 13

Exercise 13.1

Combine the two clauses, with the first as a matrix and the second as a relative clause. Make sure that you indicate by the punctuation whether the clause is restrictive or nonrestrictive.

1. Their present house is on Cranberry Road. They bought it last year.

   Their present house, which they bought last year, is on Cranberry Road.

2. Teenagers should have their driver's licenses revoked. Some teenagers are arrested for curfew violations.

   Teenagers who (that) are arrested for curfew violations should have their driver's licenses revoked.

3. Someone stole the money. They were to pay the rent with the money.

   Someone stole the money with which they were to pay the rent. (. . . the money [that/which/Ø] they were to pay the rent with)

4. The product is unsafe. This company manufactures the product.

   The product (that/which/Ø) this company manufactures is unsafe.

5. The people have now left the neighborhood. The letter is addressed to those people.

   The people to whom the letter is addressed have now left the neighborhood (the people[that/who(m)/Ø] the letter is addressed to).

6. Georgian is an inflected language of considerable complexity. Georgian is a member of the Kartvelian or South Caucasian language family.

   Georgian, which is a member of the Kartvelian or South Caucasian language family, is an inflected language of considerable complexity.

7. Human infants pass through a short critical period. They learn the basic structures of language during this period.

   Human infants pass through a short critical period during which they learn the basic structures of language.

8. I have grown tired of my old stereo. I bought my old stereo twelve years ago.

   I have grown tired of my old stereo, which I bought twelve years ago.

9. There were many voters. Many voters disapproved of the NAFTA treaty.

   There were many voters who disapproved of the NAFTA treaty.

10. They awarded the person a prize. The needle pointed at a person.

    They awarded the person at whom the needle pointed a prize. (. . . the person [that/who(m),Ø] the needle pointed at . . .)

Exercise 13.2

Diagram:

1. The guest whose watch was stolen left the party.

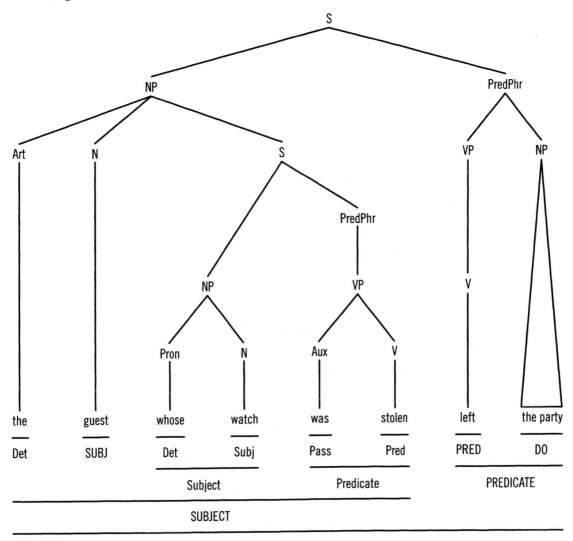

2. A light appeared from the direction in which they were looking.

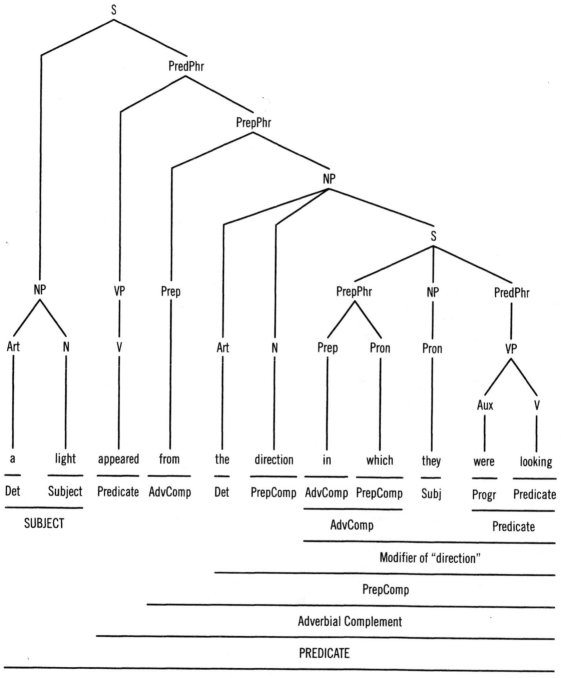

3. A stranger has identified the woman the police arrested.

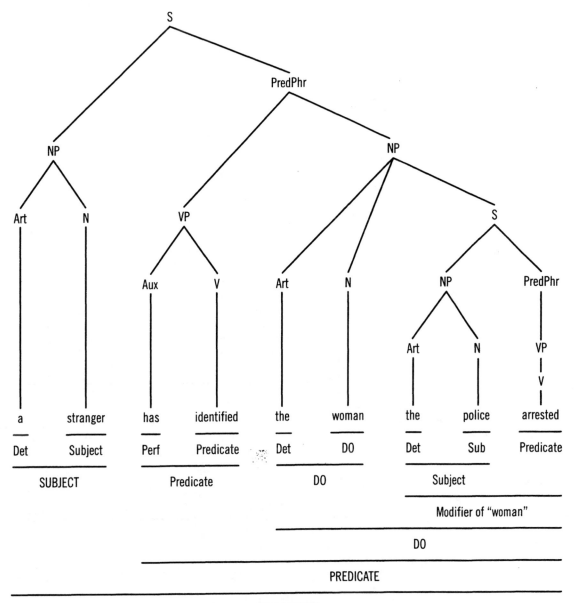

4. The house where Beethoven lived can be visited on weekdays.

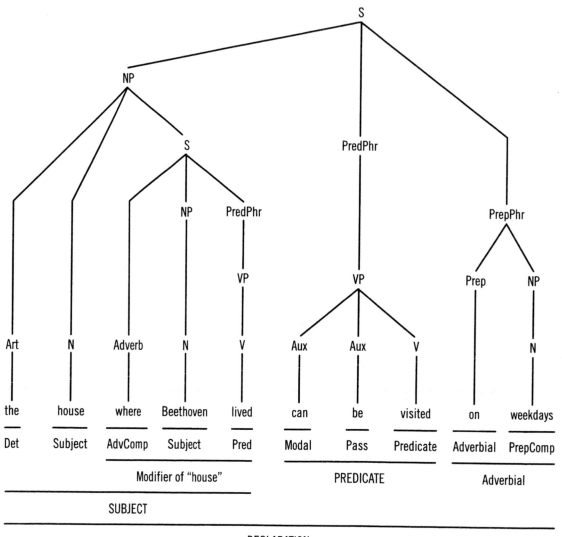

DECLARATION

Exercise 13.3

Identify and punctuate the nonrestrictive clauses.

1. The recession will benefit the public universities whose tuition fees are heavily subsidized by the state.

   The recession will benefit the public universities, whose tuition fees are heavily subsidized by the state. (nonrestrictive)

2. Many middle-class parents who had themselves attended Ivy League schools began looking closely at smaller colleges for their children.

   Many middle-class parents who had themselves attended Ivy League schools began looking closely at smaller colleges for their children. (restrictive)

3. Many voters sympathized with the poor and unemployed who had gained little from the tax break.

   Many voters sympathized with the poor and unemployed, who had gained little from the tax break. (nonrestrictive)

4. Academic departments which did not pay attention to the changing needs of the students soon found their enrollments slipping.

   Academic departments which did not pay attention to the changing needs of the students soon found their enrollments slipping. (restrictive)

5. The airplane and the motorized sled which had been introduced in the second decade of the century revolutionized the exploration of the Arctic environment.

   The airplane and the motorized sled, which had been introduced in the second decade of the century, revolutionized the exploration of the Arctic environment. (nonrestrictive)

6. Medical science began searching for the key to the control of cholesterol high levels of which were associated with heart disease.

   Medical science began searching for the key to the control of cholesterol, high levels of which were associated with heart disease. (nonrestrictive)

7. Those newspapers which had at first cautiously endorsed the plan now raised critical voices against it.

   Those newspapers which had at first cautiously endorsed the plan now raised critical voices against it. (restrictive)

8. The nightclub refused to admit customers who wore leather or other punk garb.

   The nightclub refused to admit customers who wore leather or other punk garb. (restrictive)

9. Their new car which had been left outside in front of the house all night was now covered with a generous layer of snow.

   Their new car, which had been left outside in front of the house all night, was now covered with a generous layer of snow. (nonrestrictive)

10. The president was now working fourteen-hour days which alarmed the White House doctors.

    The president was now working fourteen-hour days, which alarmed the White House doctors. (nonrestrictive)

Exercise 13.4

Which of the following sentences contain relative pronouns in clauses modifying a head noun (see 13.9)?

1. She will inherit the business on the day when she graduates.
2. I asked the gardener why our rhododendrons had all died.
3. Have you found out where the demonstration is to take place?
4. The place where they spilled the mixture had turned yellow.
5. The Fourth of July, when we celebrate our independence, is a national holiday.
6. None of us could remember where we had read the story.
7. They did not understand why so many voters had stayed away.
8. The new software can tell us how to calculate the exchange rate.
9. The district where the assaults occurred has been placed under a curfew.
10. We learned from the answering machine when Mr. Harmsworth had left the apartment.

Answers: (1), (4), (5), (9)

Exercise 14.1

Put the correct form of *who/whom* in the blanks. The sentences include examples of both noun clauses and relative clauses.

1. The players _____ reached the semi-finals were rewarded with Orange County bonds.
2. They will promote _____ ever makes the highest sales in July.
3. They have fired the designers _____ they blamed for the failure.
4. _____ ever the court names as executor will decide on the partition of the estate.
5. Some newspaper columnists criticize _____ ever they wish to discredit.
6. _____ had drawn a pumpkin head on the principal's door was never determined.
7. No one was sure _____ the committee would nominate.

8. The chief trombonist, _____ had recently joined the orchestra, was waving to his mother in the audience.

9. _____ ever wrote this article should be thrown off the Brooklyn Bridge.

10. The police officers _____ have been taking bribes will be suspended.

(1) who, (2) who, (3) whom, (4) whom, (5) whom, (6) who, (7) whom, (8) who, (9) who, (10) who

Exercise 14.2

Complete the matrix sentence with a subordinate (noun or relative) clause using the subordinator indicated in parentheses. Identify the subordinator as an internal or an external subordinator.

1. I asked Jack _____. (if)
2. The reporters _____ were forced to disclose their sources. (who)
3. All the new recruits wondered ____. (which)
4. ____ was a question on many people's minds. (whether)
5. No one could possibly imagine ____. (what)
6. Many people have disputed the claim ____. (which)
7. It was hardly surprising ____. (that)
8. _____ remained a mystery. (who)
9. The suggestion _____ amazed the brothers. (that)
10. The trophy _____ had been stolen. (that)

Possible answers:

1. *I asked Jack if he was ready. (external)*
2. *The reporters who had accused us were forced to disclose their sources. (internal)*
3. *All the new recruits wondered which company had been selected. (internal)*
4. *Whether the fuel would last the entire journey was a question on many people's minds. (external)*
5. *No one could possibly imagine what the tour guide meant by such a remark. (internal)*
6. *Many people have disputed the claim which Peary made. (internal)*
7. *It was hardly surprising that the media ignored the story. (external)*
8. *Who had informed the coast guard remained a mystery. (internal)*
9. *The suggestion that the painting was valuable amazed the brothers. (external)*
10. *The trophy that had been lent to the club had been stolen. (internal)*

Exercise 14.3

Draw a complete form-function diagram of each of the following sentences (do not use the triangle convention):

Despite the instruction not to use the triangle convention, space limitations on the printed page make it necessary to do so here and in most diagrams involving complex sentences. Students should nonetheless be required to draw complete diagrams whenever this is part of the instructions. Supplementary comments have been added to diagrams where triangles may hide important detail.

1. Ted declared that his neighborhood had been invaded by wealthy outsiders from Philadelphia.

*Comment: The abbreviation Czr stands for Complementizer; the **been** in **had been invaded** is the passive auxiliary; **from Philadelphia** is a prepositional phrase modifying **outsiders**.*

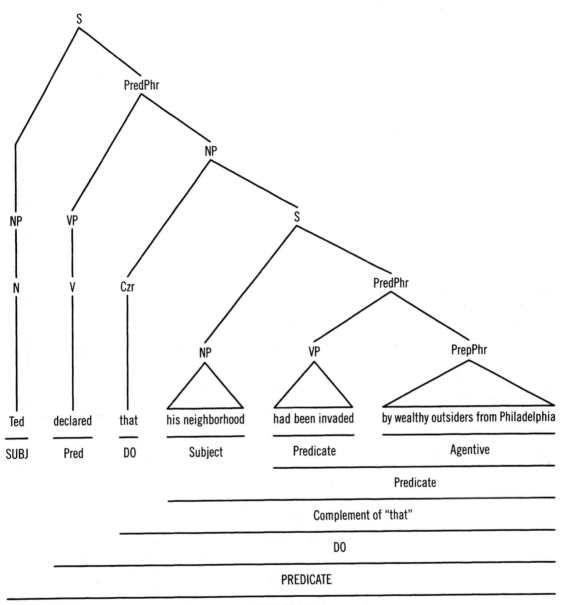

Ted	declared	that	his neighborhood	had been invaded	by wealthy outsiders from Philadelphia
SUBJ	Pred	DO	Subject	Predicate	Agentive

Predicate

Complement of "that"

DO

PREDICATE

DECLARATION

2. That the man who had climbed the fence was deranged was obvious.

*Comment: **had** is the auxiliary of the perfect aspect.*

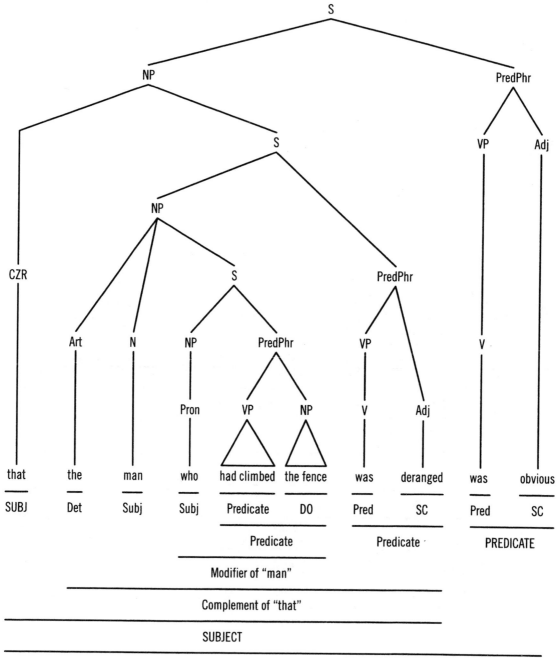

Exercise 14.4

Rewrite these sentences using extraposition with *it* in the subject position.

1. That the aliens would invade Earth on Halloween seemed plausible to many scientists.

   It seemed plausible to many scientists that the aliens would invade Earth on Halloween.

2. How they had gained access to the safe was not clear.

   It was not clear how they had gained access to the safe.

3. Why "hardly" should trigger adverb-operator inversion was a big mystery to grammarians.

   It was a big mystery to grammarians why "hardly" should trigger adverb-operator inversion.

4. Whether the demonstration could be stopped by force was doubtful.

   It was doubtful whether the demonstration could be stopped by force.

5. How the mass jail break was planned was baffling to the investigators.

   It was baffling to the investigators how the mass jail break was planned.

6. That the professors had voted themselves a big salary increase was recorded in the minutes.

   It was recorded in the minutes that the professors had voted themselves a big salary increase.

7. Exactly how the Action Party had funded their campaign was revealed by one of the local newspapers.

   It was revealed by one of the local newspapers exactly how the Action Party had funded their campaign.

8. How many people were taken in by the New York Sunshine scam was tragic.

   It was tragic how many people were taken in by the New York Sunshine scam.

9. Whether the grammar exam would include a question on extraposition was irrelevant to the students.

   It was irrelevant to the students whether the grammar exam would include a question on extraposition.

10. When the demonstration was scheduled was made known by posters.

    It was made known by posters when the demonstration was scheduled.

EXERCISE ANSWERS: CHAPTER 15

Exercise 15.1

Replace the blank space in the first sentence with the entire second sentence, using a full clause or a partial clause (gerund or infinitive), whichever is indicated.

1. Trilby accused them of _____. They put soy sauce in the vegetable ragout. (partial)

   Trilby accused them of putting soy sauce in the vegetable ragout.

2. Yeoville suspects _____. The FBI has planted a tape recorder in his refrigerator. (full)

   Yeoville suspects that the FBI has planted a tape recorder in his refrigerator.

3. _____ would have made the headlines. Fenworth sailed the *Albatross* across the Pacific in ten days. (partial)

   For Fenworth to have sailed the Albatross *across the Pacific in ten days would have made the headlines.*

4. Mattie pretended _____. He had locked them out of the house. (partial)

   Mattie pretended to have locked them out of the house.

5. I do not know _____. Are you serious or not? (full)

   I do not know whether you are serious or not.

6. The workers were asking _____. What is the real annual income of the CEOs? (full)

   The workers were asking what the real annual income of the CEOs was.

7. They asked the farmer _____. May we put up our tents in this field? (full)

   They asked the farmer whether they might put up their tents in her field.

8. The graduate students objected to _____. They must pay fees for undergraduate-only events. (partial)

   The graduate students objected to having to pay fees for undergraduate-only events.

9. The hikers were overjoyed at _____. They could change out of their wet clothes. (partial)

   The hikers were overjoyed at being able to change out of their wet clothes.

10. I must ask _____. Can we afford this extravagance? (full)

I must ask whether we can afford this extravagance.

Exercise 15.2

Convert the following sentences into NPs, using first the gerund, then the infinitive construction, and make each NP the subject of the predicate supplied in parentheses. Example:

John complained to the management about the staff's attitude. (was surprising)

    a. John's complaining to the management about the staff's attitude was surprising. (gerund)

    b. For John to complain to the management about the staff's attitude was surprising. (infinitive)

1. The patriots flew the Ruritanian flag. *(required considerable courage)*

    a. The patriots' flying the Ruritanian flag required considerable courage.

    b. For the patriots to have flown the Ruritanian flag required considerable courage.

2. All those children did well in the tests. *(is to the credit of the School Board)*

    a. All those children's doing well in the tests is to the credit of the School Board.

    b. For all those children to have done well in the tests is to the credit of the School Board.

3. The government has sold the landowners the mineral rights. *(scandalized the voters)*

    a. The government's selling the landowners the mineral rights scandalized the voters.

    b. For the government to have sold the landowners the mineral rights scandalized the voters.

4. The agency has been listening to our phone conversations. *(would be a violation of our constitutional rights)*

    a. The agency's having been listening to our phone conversations. (would be a violation of our constitutional rights)

    b. For the agency to have been listening to our phone conversations would be a violation of our constitutional rights.

5. You must be available at all times. *(is a requirement of the job)*

    a. Your having to be available at all times is a requirement of the job.

    b. For you to have to be available at all times is a requirement of the job.

6. She will become chief financial officer. *(will calm the frantic stockholders)*

a. *Her becoming chief financial officer will calm the frantic stockholders.*

b. *For her to become chief financial officer will calm the frantic stockholders.*

7. The power company was building a dam in the mountains. *(worried the environmentalists)*

a. *The power company's building a dam in the mountains worried the environmentalists.*

b. *For the power company to be building a dam in the mountains worried the environmentalists.*

8. Rudy contacted the foreman of the jury. *(would have resulted in a mistrial)*

a. *Rudy's contacting the foreman of the jury would have resulted in a mistrial.*

b. *For Rudy to have contacted the foreman of the jury would have resulted in a mistrial.*

9. The Dow-Jones average fell despite the low inflation rate. *(alarmed many investors)*

a. *The Dow-Jones average's having fallen despite the low inflation rate alarmed many investors.*

b. *For the Dow-Jones average to have fallen despite the low inflation rate alarmed many investors.*

10. The district attorney takes the rumors seriously. *(is evidence of his stupidity)*

a. *The district attorney's taking the rumors seriously is evidence of his stupidity.*

b. *For the district attorney to take the rumors seriously is evidence of his stupidity.*

Exercise 15.3

Make the sentences inside quotation marks into reported speech, using the matrix clause suggested in the parentheses.

1. "The army is leaving us unprotected" (The refugees complained to the commissioner)

   The refugees complained to the commissioner that the army was leaving them unprotected.

2. "I am innocent of this charge" (The defendant continued to insist)

   The defendant continued to insist that she was innocent of that charge.

3. "I had already turned on the lights when he attacked me" (The witness testified)

   The witness testified that she had already turned on the lights when he attacked her.

4. "Did you arrive here yesterday?" (Ms. Bridges asked Jenny)

   Ms. Bridges asked Jenny whether she had arrived there yesterday.

5. "Our travel agent told us the museum would be open every day this week" (The tourists complained to the Visitors' Bureau)

   The tourists complained to the Visitors' Bureau that their travel agent had told them the museum would be open every day that week.

6. "If you had bought tickets for both of us, I could have sold mine at the entrance" (Jill said to her boyfriend)

   Jill said to her boyfriend that if he had bought tickets for both of them, she could have sold hers at the entrance.

7. "I was born and grew up in this house, and by God I am going to die here!" (General Bordwehr declared)

   General Bordwehr declared he had been born and had grown up in that house, and by God he was going to die there!

8. "We mailed the parcel yesterday from this very post office" (Mrs. Tucker testified)

   Mrs. Tucker testified that they had mailed the parcel the previous day from that very post office.

9. "I told Jack the news as soon as I returned from the hospital" (John assured Lisa)

   John assured Lisa that he had told Jack the news as soon as he, John, returned from the hospital.

10. "Do not return their passports until they have signed the declaration" (The chief of police ordered the customs officials)

    The chief of police ordered the customs officials that they should not return their passports until they had signed the declaration. (Or: . . . not to return their passports until they had signed the declaration.)

Exercise 15.4

Identify any noun clauses or relative clauses in the following sentences. Indicate any examples of subordinate clauses that could be either.

1. The fierce determination that we could perceive on the part of the rebels made us anxious to reach a settlement of the conflict.

   That we could perceive is a relative clause.

2. None of us believed the report that the enemy had finally submitted.

   *That the enemy had finally submitted could be either a relative clause modifying **report** or a noun clause in apposition to **report.***

3. The monumental sculptures sprang from her deep desire that her work should not be forgotten.

   That her work should not be forgotten is a noun clause.

4. The announcement that the concert had been canceled was greeted with boos and catcalls.

   That the concert had been canceled is a noun clause.

5. The warning that one out of three citizens would be audited greatly increased tax compliance.

   That one out of three citizens would be audited is a noun clause.

6. Most of the inhabitants ignored the proclamation that had been issued the previous day.

   That had been issued the previous day is a relative clause.

7. The story that the supposedly deaf conspirators could hear made the judge angry.

   *That the supposedly deaf conspirators could hear could be either a relative clause modifying **story** or a noun clause in apposition to **story**.*

8. The swim team listened to the advice that the coach was giving them.

   That the coach was giving them is a relative clause.

9. The agreement that the union was about to negotiate with the management bolstered the stock market.

   *That the union was about to negotiate with the management could be a relative clause modifying **agreement**, or, although this is somewhat less likely, a noun clause in apposition to **agreement**.*

10. Much of the research was motivated by a deep belief that nonhuman creatures could not acquire language.

    That nonhuman creatures could not acquire language is a noun clause.

Exercise 15.5

(For class discussion) The adjective *concerned* can appear in two distinct contexts, as illustrated by

1. The social worker is concerned that he take his medication regularly.

2. The social worker is concerned that he drinks too much alcohol.

After analyzing the two sentences, what can you say about the two meanings of "concerned" and the way the meaning affects the grammar?

*The subordinate clause in (1), **that he take his medication regularly**, has* *the verb in the subjunctive. The subordinate clause* **that he drinks too much alcohol** *in (2) has the verb in the -s present.*

One of the meanings of **concerned** *is simple attention to or worry about a state of affairs, without a necessary suggestion that the subject is actively involved. The other suggests that the subject is involved in trying to change or maintain a situation, especially by controlling the actions of someone else. The second of these meanings requires the subjunctive in the subordinate clause, as in* **he take** *in sentence (1).*

EXERCISE ANSWERS: CHAPTER 16

Exercise 16.1

Identify the function of *where* or *when* in each of the following sentences as (i) complementizer for adverbial clause or noun clause, (ii) relative pronoun, or (iii) *wh*-subordinator for noun clause.

1. I asked them where they had hidden the gloves.
2. Unscrupulous dealers sold the icons in the West, where museums did not always ask questions.
3. Assistance can sometimes be obtained from the federal government when financial support for small businesses is not available locally.
4. Mr. Edgeworth was late for the meeting where the firm's bankruptcy was announced.
5. The stretch of rail where the accident had occurred had not been checked by the engineers.
6. An e-mail message informed us when the lecture would take place.
7. We especially enjoyed the place in his autobiography where he discussed his first marriage.
8. When the fourth earthquake hit, the family decided to move back to Rhode Island.
9. Gilbert knew of a restaurant where they served vegetarian food.
10. We remembered the last occasion when Ms. Redfern invited us to lunch.

(1) wh-subordinator, (2) relative pronoun, (3) complementizer, (4) relative pronoun, (5) relative pronoun, (6) wh-subordinator, (7) relative pronoun, (8) complementizer, (9) relative pronoun, (10) relative pronoun

Exercise 16.2

Identify the function of *if* as (i) conditional, (ii) concessive, or (iii) complementizer for noun clause.

1. If our boat is small, it is nonetheless seaworthy.
2. I asked them if he could come with us.
3. If the blizzard dies down, we can continue our journey.
4. We would be obliged if you would write a letter to your member of Congress supporting our position.
5. If you think your government is an overblown bureaucracy, you should live for a year in Ruritania.
6. None of us could discover if they really believed in the existence of Bigfoot.
7. The union organizers would be pleased if the rank-and-file members found a cause to fight for.
8. The attorney asked if anyone had already seen the will.
9. If the verb is transitive, its subject must have the ergative case suffix.
10. If conditions in the federal penitentiary are grim, they are better than those in the county jail.

(1) concessive, (2) complementizer, (3) conditional, (4) conditional, (5) conditional, (6) complementizer, (7) conditional, (8) complementizer, (9) conditional, (10) concessive

Exercise 16.3

Diagram the following sentences.

1. Since your grant has been approved by the foundation, you should now apply for a leave of absence.

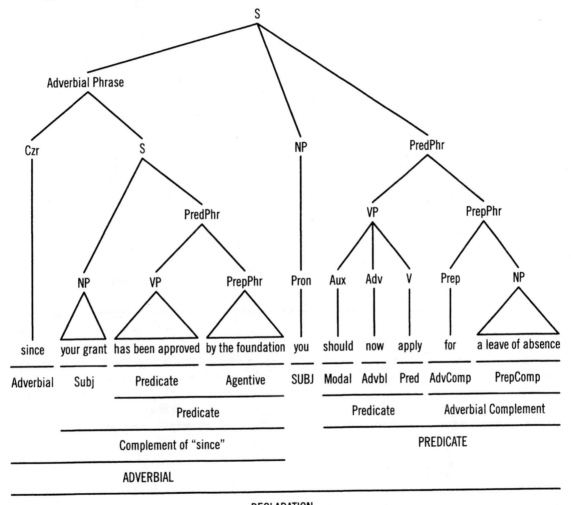

2. The firefighters could not escape because the flames had come up the valley behind them.

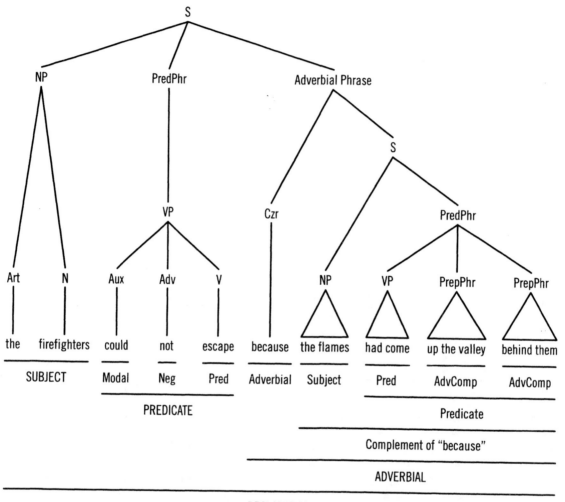

Exercise 16.4

Identify the type of adverbial clause.

1. Wherever the funny man with the flute went, he was followed by crowds of children.
2. The defense attorney objected whenever the footprints were mentioned.
3. It had rained heavily the night before, so that the field was now a quagmire.

4. Granted that we do not have the cultural opportunities of a larger city, the prosperity and neighborliness of Oldville keep our population stable.

5. The instant he said the words "property values," a hush fell over the auditorium.

6. The French horn players were placed offstage so that the music would have the distant quality the composer was striving for.

7. The negotiators cannot change this condition for the simple reason that their mandate explicitly forbids it.

8. Provided you arrive in Sacramento on the 14th, you are free to take any route you like.

9. She has argued her case well, considering she has had no legal training.

10. So as to cover themselves against a flood, they had purchased multiple policies.

(1) place, (2) time, (3) result, (4) concession, (5) time, (6) purpose, (7) reason, (8) condition, (9) concession, (10) purpose

Exercise 16.5

(For class discussion) The following sentences, which include both compound and complex sentences, are anomalous in some way. Explain the anomalies in grammatical terms. How would you improve them?

1. Although her propeller shaft had snapped and her rudder had splintered, the fishing boat was drifting helplessly in the high seas.

   *Although, a concessive subordinator, introduces a clause that in some sense contradicts the meaning of the main clause (as in "although it is raining, it is quite pleasant"). But these two clauses aren't in any sense incompatible. Quite the opposite—the first clause would explain the main clause. Change **although** to **because**, or coordinate the two clauses with **and**.*

2. That the end was lost to view over the horizon, the line of people in front of the palace was so long.

   ***That the end was lost to view over the horizon** is a result clause. Result clauses cannot precede the main clause. Reverse the order of the two clauses.*

3. The voters considered it imperative that the deficit was reduced.

   Considered it imperative** is a "control" predicate whose subordinate clause must be in the subjunctive. Change to **that the deficit be reduced.

4. Geraldine tore the page out of her diary until a faint light on the horizon heralded the dawn.

   ***Tore the page out of her diary** is a punctual event and cannot be fol-*

*lowed by an adverbial clause introduced by **until**. The sentence could be saved by making **page** plural: **tore pages out of her diary.***

5. If Lincoln lost the election, the Southern states would not have seceded.

   *An unreal condition requires the auxiliary **had**. Since, as is well known, Lincoln did not lose the election, the conditional clause must have the form **If Lincoln had lost the election** . . .*

6. If they would not have noticed the leak in time, the boat wo sunk.

   *Again, the auxiliary **had** is needed in the if-clause of an unreal (tion: **If they had not noticed** . . .*

7. If Elsie Goodenough was chair of the board, we would see a more favorable reaction from the stockholders.

   *In the conditional clause **If Elsie Goodenough was chair of the board**, the state of affairs is a possibility but not a fact. The verb must therefore be in the second subjunctive: **If Elsie Goodenough were chair of the board** . . .*

8. But the tickets were definitely missing, in desperation we searched through every inch of our suitcases.

   *The order of coordinated clauses cannot be reversed. Change to: **In desperation we searched through every inch of our suitcases, but the tickets were definitely missing.***

9. The legislators were relying on that the inflation rate would remain low.

   *Noun clauses introduced by the complementizer **that** cannot have a preposition. Change **that** to **the expectation that** or **the prospect that**.*

10. The tourists had expected visiting Angkor Wat before they left.

    *The verb **to expect** takes an infinitive rather than a gerund. Change **expected visiting** to . . . **expected to visit** . . .*

EXERCISE ANSWERS: CHAPTER 17

Exercise 17.1

Which of the following sentences contain new subjects?

1. A police detective stood in the doorway.
2. The president has decided to veto the bill.

3. We have arranged a surprise party for the graduating seniors.

4. Your guests have arrived.

5. Just before dawn a light rain began to fall.

6. The sun was shining brightly on the red roofs of the farms.

7. My parents had recently bought a summer cottage in Michigan.

8. There were several people knocking on doors in our neighborhood this morning.

9. It was the cost of renovating the damaged rooms that changed our minds.

10. The committee on nominations has asked you to stand for vice president.

1, 4, 5, 8, 9 (but one could argue that it is the subject!)

Exercise 17.2.

Convert the following sentences into (a) cleft sentences, (b) pseudocleft sentences, or (c) existential (*there is/are*) sentences, as indicated.

1. I need a few days' vacation in the Caribbean. (pseudocleft)

    What I need is a few days' vacation in the Caribbean.

2. The Republicans were more embarrassed by the incident. (cleft)

    It was the Republicans who were more embarrassed by the incident.

3. A student is waiting to see you. (existential)

    There is a student waiting to see you.

4. Several potholes are in the main street. (existential)

    There are several potholes in the main street.

5. We found that the earlier results were wrong. (pseudocleft)

    What we found was that the earlier results were wrong.

6. Toxic chemicals, not a virus, were responsible for the strange symptoms. (cleft)

    It was toxic chemicals, not a virus, that were responsible for the strange symptoms.

7. The songbird population was most seriously affected by the new fertilizers. (cleft)

    It was the songbird population that was most seriously affected by the new fertilizers.

8. By the end of the decade, no one except a few of the older villagers was still illiterate. (existential)

    By the end of the decade, there was no one except a few of the older villagers who was still illiterate.

9. Instead the government economists proposed a further tax increase. (pseudocleft)

   Instead what the government economists proposed was a further tax increase.

10. Administrative inefficiency, not the poor harvest, brought about the food shortages. (cleft)

    It was administrative inefficiency, not the poor harvest, that brought about the food shortages.

Exercise 17.3

Rephrase each of the following sentences so that, as far as possible, the principle of older and newer information is observed.

1. At his retirement party they presented a gold watch to him.

   At his retirement party they presented him with a gold watch.

2. The farmers are blaming unusually heavy rainfall in the spring for the bad harvest.

   The farmers are blaming the bad harvest on unusually heavy rainfall in the spring.

3. Manfred looked "rheostat" up.

   Manfred looked up "rheostat."

4. The sailors threw a rope tied in a bowline to me.

   The sailors threw me a rope tied in a bowline.

5. A tidal wave swamped the village in the early spring.

   In the early spring the village was swamped by a tidal wave.

6. He sold a naive realtor from the city his farm.

   He sold his farm to a naive realtor from the city.

7. They will provide board and accommodation for three nights to you.

   They will provide you with board and accommodation for three nights.

8. Mike has been teaching inner-city schoolchildren from poor families French.

   Mike has been teaching French to inner-city schoolchildren from poor families.

9. Gloria was so disgusted that she turned her resignation in.

   Gloria was so disgusted that she turned in her resignation.

10. A recount of the votes was demanded by the losing candidate.

    The losing candidate demanded a recount of the votes.

Exercise 17.4

The following opening paragraph of a story contains sentences that are formulated in ways that are inappropriate to the function they serve. Rewrite the passage so that it makes sense and reads smoothly. For example, you will need to change cleft and pseudocleft sentences, passives and actives, pronouns and nouns, and the positions of prepositional phrases. (Do not, however, change the order of the sentences.)

A king of Ruritania once was, and three sons were had by him. The oldest son, Prince Gerald, was the crown prince. In the army through his own merit the oldest son, Prince Gerald, became a senior officer. It was the daughter of a high-ranking courtier that the oldest son had married and what they had was several children. Prince Gerald traveled widely in his youth, and many modern ideas were brought to Ruritania by Prince Gerald. There was the second son, Prince Gundolf, who was a quiet man with intellectual interests, and it was he who painted. What was played by him was the flute, and books on literature and philosophy were read by the second son, Prince Gundolf. The second son, Prince Gundolf, had a pleasant and humane disposition. Although the crown prince, Prince Gerald, the oldest son, was much admired by the people, he was the best loved by the people. But if the two older sons were successful, the youngest son was a wastrel and a drunkard. Prince Garth, the youngest son, was a constant embarrassment to the king and to his brothers, and the courtiers despised Prince Garth. When on maneuvers Gerald was away, and what Gundolf was engrossed in establishing was museums, art galleries, and universities, after for days at a time in the taverns of the cities the youngest son, Prince Garth, had disappeared, a sodden wreck, the youngest son would return.

There was once a king of Ruritania, and he had three sons. The oldest son, Prince Gerald, was the crown prince. He went into the army at an early age and became a senior officer through his own merit. He married the daughter of a high-ranking courtier, and they had several children. Prince Gerald traveled widely in his youth and brought many modern ideas to Ruritania. The second son, Prince Gundolf, was a quiet man with intellectual interests, who painted, played the flute, and read books on literature and philosophy. He had a pleasant and humane disposition. Although the crown prince was much admired by the people, it was Prince Gundolf who was most loved. But if the two older sons were successful, the youngest son, Prince Garth, was a wastrel and a drunkard. He was a constant embarrassment to the king and to his brothers, and was despised by the courtiers. When Gerald was away on maneuvers, and Gundolf was engrossed in establishing museums, art galleries, and universities, Garth would disappear for days at a time in the taverns of the cities and return a sodden wreck.